26, 27, 82, 84-85

Speaker's Corner Books

is a provocative new series designed to stimulate, educate, and foster discussion on significant public policy topics. Written by experts in a variety of fields, these brief and engaging books should be read by anyone interested in the trends and issues that shape our society.

More thought-provoking titles
in the Speaker's Corner series

Think for Yourself!
An Essay on Cutting through the Babble, the Bias, and the Hype
  Steve Hindes

The Enduring Wilderness:
Protecting Our Natural Heritage through the Wilderness Act
  Doug Scott

Parting Shots from My Brittle Bow:
Reflections on American Politics and Life
  Eugene J. McCarthy

The Brave New World of Health Care
  Richard D. Lamm

Social Security and the Golden Age:
An Essay on the New American Demographic
  George McGovern

For more information visit our Web site
  www.fulcrum-books.com

God and Caesar in America

an Essay on Religion and Politics

Gary Hart

Former Senator and Best-Selling Author

Fulcrum Publishing

Golden, Colorado

Text copyright © 2005 Gary Hart

Library of Congress Cataloging-in-Publication Data

Hart, Gary, 1936-
  God and Caesar in America : an essay on religion and politics / by Gary Hart.
      p. cm.
  ISBN 1-55591-577-9 (pbk.)
  1. Christianity and politics--United States. 2. Religion and politics—United States. 3. Religious right—United States. 4. United States—Religion. I. Title.
  BR115.P7H356 2005
  322'.1'0973—dc22

                          2005020876

ISBN10 1-55591-577-9   ISBN13 978-1-55591-577-3
Printed in the United States of America
0 9 8 7 6 5 4 3 2 1

Editorial: Sam Scinta, Faith Marcovecchio
Cover image and design: Jack Lenzo

We have just enough religion to make us hate,
But not enough to make us love one another.
—Jonathan Swift

Contents

The Political Revival of the Religious Right

America in the early twenty-first century is witnessing a religious revival. Exactly how widespread it is, how long it will last, or what its true root causes are is not yet clear. This is by no means the first religious revival in America. At irregular intervals, and for disparate reasons, religious revivals occur. An instinct for apocalypse, a resort to spirituality, attendance at worship, and the search for meaning have characterized these movements. They have waxed, and they have waned. It is safe to say, however, that the early twenty-first-century wave of religious concern is more overtly political than any in American history.

Given the history and culture of the United States, the twenty-first-century religious awakening is overwhelmingly Christian, and, within the Christian church, overwhelmingly Protestant, and, within Protestantism, overwhelmingly evangelical, and, within the broad evangelical tradition, overwhelmingly fundamentalist. Thus, it would be more precise to say: there is a Protestant fundamentalist evangelical religious revival in America today that has become highly political. In the last decade or so attendance has been up in evangelical churches and new, nondenominational community churches even while participation and membership remain on a plateau or are in decline in Catholic churches and mainline, traditional Protestant denominations.

It should be noted, however, that the fundamentalist

Protestant revival attracts fundamentalist Catholic support on abortion and life-maintenance issues, though Catholics generally have not joined the apocalyptic "end of days" aspect of the revival. It should also be noted that a wave of fundamentalism arose in several major religions— Christianity, Judaism, and Islam—following the end of the Cold War, but there is little indication of any dramatic upsurge in devotion in American Judaism or Muslim communities.

Scholars of American religious history find various causes for the phenomenon of religious revivals. Usually they occur during economic crises such as depressions and deep recessions with mass unemployment and uncertainty over the means of livelihood, or they are apocalyptic risings occasioned by dramatic natural events, catastrophic occurrences, or the possibility of nuclear annihilation. More likely religious revivals are brought on by a sense of moral decay and the fear of social collapse. Sometimes one fear contributes to another.

Today there is relative economic stability, though globalization and the information revolution have introduced Schumpeter's "gales of creative destruction" and the end of the Cold War has dramatically reduced the chance of nuclear war. Nevertheless, the cultural revolution of the 1960s, the infamous age of sex, drugs, and rock-and-roll, marked for some the beginning of the end of traditional American society and culture, a society based on family and community and a culture based on wholesome entertainment, amateur sports, and sublimated sexual behavior.

With the 1960s came racial and gender revolutions, integration of schools and communities, women and black Americans competing for white male jobs, the beginning of the disintegration of the traditional American family, one-parent households, high divorce rates, for a period of time greatly increased crime rates, political protests and occasional violence in the streets, the decline of small-town America and the expansion of urban then suburban populations, and a revolution in music, movies, and television that clashed with "traditional American values."

Those concerned with the long-term implications of these collective trends and the deep uncertainties and instabilities they created began to preach and mobilize support against them. To start the great pendulum of cultural evolution swinging back in the direction of tradition, apocalyptic rhetoric has often been employed. One can see the image of the perennial *New Yorker* cartoon character, always bearded, long-haired, and white-robe-clad, bearing his ubiquitous sign "The End Is Near." And for some, though not all, revivalists, all this upheaval does signal the end of days. Thus the massive success of apocalyptic book series and the movie *The Passion of the Christ*. For those on the apocalyptic side of the scale, the emergence of the signs and symbols of the Book of Revelations strongly suggests that it is time to get one's spiritual house in order and to prepare for the end, when the saved and the damned will be forever parted.

For those on the other side of the scale of revival, those who do not necessarily see the end of days, at least not quite yet, there is one more chance, one more possibility to set things right, to return America to its traditional and true course before the social and cultural revolutions of the second half of the twentieth century put it, at least metaphorically, on the road to hell. To create a counterrevolution requires rallying like-minded people. In the religious revival of the early twenty-first century, it also requires becoming active politically to seek to legislate reversal of the perceived destructive forces.

The rise of the revivalist right and cultural conservatism

is a direct result of several decades of social and cultural upheaval. Adoption of the cause of civil rights and passage of civil rights legislation in the 1960s turned almost all of the American South from conservative Democratic to conservative Republican. Interestingly, the civil rights cause was one strongly supported by mainstream

The rise of the revivalist right and cultural conservatism is a direct result of several decades of social and cultural upheaval.

Protestant churches and many Jewish and Catholic activists. The feminist movement and the entry of women into the workplace, starting during World War II but dramatically increasing in the 1960s and 1970s, the subsequent rise in divorce rates and fragmentation of families, and the socially divisive demand for abortion rights and then gay rights helped turn small-town America from fiscally conservative to culturally conservative and contributed to the shifting of a large portion of the male population from moderate to conservative. The rise of gun violence and the subsequent effort to control gun sales and register gun ownership turned traditionally independent westerners into hard-rock conservatives and some into antigovernment right-wingers and radical militia members. To cap it off, the tide of sex and violence and the increased vulgarization of the entertainment industry created widespread loathing, if not also fear, across the political spectrum, including among those who continued to listen to the sinful music and watch the corrupting programs.

As all these social and cultural shifts began to represent a giant pendulum swinging politically rightward, those organizing the counterrevolution were also seeking meaning and solace in the shelter of the church, and not just any church but the Protestant evangelical church offered purpose, stability, and shelter from the vulgar, meaningless chaos that seemed to characterize late-twentieth-century American society. These churches counsel families to stay together; they offer training in traditional Christian values to children; they provide music, social programs, and wholesome entertainment not just on Sundays but throughout the week for the whole family. Community churches are filling a huge vacuum in society.

Waves of social change rarely are accidental or occur outside some historic context. The Cold War defined the second half of the twentieth century. Like America's participation in the defeat of imperialism in World War I and its leadership in the defeat of fascism in World War II, the Cold War was premised on an ideological struggle between democracy and communism, and its central organizing principle was containment of communism. Thus, the entire twentieth century was characterized by the clash of ideologies or systems of political belief. But the Cold War ended abruptly, and a massive political vacuum, filled quickly by radical fundamentalism, ethnic nationalism, and tribalism, was created. If our principle purpose in the world was to contain communism and communism has collapsed, who are we now and what is our purpose? What can we now believe in?

To add to the uncertainty for middle- and upper-income classes, the limits of materialism as a driving force were being reached. If every room has a television, every high school student has a car, every closet is full of clothes, and every supermarket has a bewildering array of food choices, what else is there? Soon came the leveling force of exposé journalism, which pulled away any cloak of distance or mystery from political leadership, first humanizing then diminishing it: if every failure is a "scandal," who can be trusted? Finally, mass mobility and the erosion of small-town and neighborhood life left a vacuum where traditional communities used to be. The end of the twentieth century represented a social revolution on multiple levels—the end of ideology, the limits of materialism, the diminishment of leadership, the loss of community—that practically begged for political response.

And political response was soon to come. One thing is certain in modern American politics, particularly a politics driven by pollsters, focus groups, and professional consultants, and that is that tidal shifts in society represent a gold mine, a new source of political wealth, to be worked and plundered. Skillful conservative analysts possessing delicate and sensitive political Richter monitors, finely calibrated instruments that can detect political earthquakes even before they occur, tapped into this massive energy shift while traditional liberals rested on the laurels of the New Deal and the Great Society, their majorities in Congress and mayors in great cities, and their familiar coalition of labor unions and minorities, liberated women and environmentalists. Not only did conservative political managers make common cause with the evangelical movement, even when sophisticates ridiculed its more steamy and seamy televangelist preachers, they sought a convenient demon upon which to pin all the blames of a troubled nation. This is a tactic common to all crusades. They began a drumbeat that pinned the nation's grievances and woes on "Liberals." And soon all

> The end of the twentieth century represented a social revolution on multiple levels—the end of ideology, the limits of materialism, the diminishment of leadership, the loss of community—that practically begged for a political response.

Democrats were liberals and all liberals were to blame for all ills, real and perceived, in our society.

Tired of shoddy and embarrassing entertainment? It's the liberals' fault. Do you think America is off the track? Blame the liberals. Lost your job? The liberals, who favor trade, did it. Afraid of urban gangs invading your neighborhood, even in small-town Colorado? The liberals are weak on law enforcement. Tired of paying taxes to support welfare bums? It's the liberal social programs that have created a huge giveaway system. On it went and on it still goes. Time, however, has a way of setting things right. Given conservative control of government power long enough and given a pretty continuous size of government, level of taxes (or rise of deficits), seediness of entertainment, perpetuation of social ills, and the blame game will eventually run its course.

In the meantime, the question of the relationship of religion, particularly evangelical religion, to politics remains. It is not a new question. It preoccupied America's founders from the beginning if for no other reason than that many of them or their forbearers left their European homes to escape religious persecution and to worship—or not worship—as they pleased. They did not want an official, or even unofficial, state religion. They also did not want the state to tell them that they could not worship. And they did not want the president or the Congress to tell them that they had to worship. They wanted the church and the state to be separate, and they said so explicitly—"Congress shall make no law respecting an establishment of religion"—using language that leaves little room for interpretation.

This language, of course, neither encouraged nor discouraged religion or religious belief. Nor was it meant to preclude religious revival. It simply meant that the state, the government, should stay out of it, neither encouraging nor discouraging religious practice and belief. This language also did not preclude or even discourage individual politicians from discussing their religious beliefs if they chose to. What neither they, nor their parties, nor the government could do, however, was to impose their beliefs on others by law, regulation, or official acts of government. As it has often been said, the constitutional separation of church and state was not intended to protect the state from the church but to protect the church from the state. Those founders insistent on a Bill of Rights would be the first to warn modern political evangelists to be careful about imposing the church on the state because of the inevitable danger that the state will eventually impose itself on the church.

But, when the Supreme Court ruled that a woman had a personal right to determine whether to have an abortion, was not that the "government" imposing its beliefs on those who disagreed? When courts, both federal and state, permitted family members to withdraw life-sustaining treatment from brain-dead patients, was not that the "government" violating profound religious beliefs regarding the sanctity of life? When teenage women could receive advice on reproduction and contraceptive devices, was not that the introduction of a policy that violated freedom of religion? Did not these and many other social steps of the late twentieth century involving profound religious beliefs on the part of Protestant evangelical, conservative, and Catholic churches mean that the "government" was making laws, or at least condoning laws, respecting the establishment of religion?

These were legal and political decisions, but they profoundly affected the religious beliefs of many people, people who were quickly invited to join conservative political parties and causes designed to reverse trends they perceived to be evil. To them, the problem was not the government promoting religion; the problem was the government actively attacking religious beliefs. This, they believed, had to be stopped. There was a point, in the judgment of religious conservatives, where a constitutionally secular society was becoming corrupt, iniquitous, and wicked and thus on the road to self-destruction, that is unless it was rescued by a religious revival that would restore "faith" and traditional social values.

For the Jeffersonians among us, it is important that attention be paid. It is too easy to oppose, to ridicule, or to dismiss voices seeking to be heard simply because managers of one particular party, in this case the conservative party, have skillfully opened their arms to this movement and turned it to their purposes. Surely there are dangers in the theocratic tendencies of any groups in our society seeking to impose, by legislation or court packing, their religious beliefs on all the rest of us. This is particularly true when the cynical political manipulators construct extreme political alliances, say among Protestant fundamentalists, extreme Israeli sects, or dissident fundamentalist Catholics. Such actions are nothing but the calculated distillation and energizing of extreme views for the purposes of wielding political power. To truly understand the current religious revival, its motivations and causes must be separated from the destructive political manipulations to which it has succumbed and its legitimate grievances must be considered and addressed, not casually dismissed.

For purposes of this essay, I make a sharp distinction between traditional, mainstream, and established faiths and one wing of evangelical Protestantism that has undertaken to wage a political crusade to impose its beliefs on the nation at large. The vast majority of the faithful of any religion are zealous, not in order to dictate through the political process, but to preserve their faith and its practices from usurpation by politics or the conversion of their systems of worship into political instruments. This essay, therefore, is not a discussion of the relationship between religion and politics in the abstract or in a theoretical sense, but is instead a critical analysis of the dangers of one minority wing of one religion subverting one party, and eventually the political system, to its beliefs. And, likewise, it is a discussion of the cynical use by political manipulators of a religious revival to ensure political power.

Those of us who have roots in both evangelical Protestantism and Jeffersonian democratic republicanism should not sit on the sidelines sadly shaking our heads at the chaos created by this unhappy clash between two American traditions and simply decrying the political cynicism seeking to capitalize upon it. But to find a better course, one with nobler ideals and humanitarian purposes, each of us must first qualify ourselves to speak.

In my own case, that qualification involves roots in two traditions not considered compatible in the political-religious wars of the early twenty-first century.

One Man's Faith and a Life of Public Service

From childhood through college, my religious training and my higher education took place in the Church of the Nazarene in Ottawa, Kansas, and Bethany, Oklahoma. Founded around 1905, the Church of the Nazarene was created by ministers and laypeople who separated themselves from the Methodist Church in America. The detailed history of this schism is not particularly relevant to this discussion. It is sufficient to say that the Nazarenes believe in two works of grace: salvation (which today is popularly referred to as being born again) and sanctification, the purification of the heart and spirit and the dedication of one's life to the service to God. In the early and mid-twentieth century, and largely so still today, Nazarenes believed in strict personal conduct and the rejection of "worldly" behavior such as movie-going, dancing, gambling, the use of alcohol and tobacco, female adornment with cosmetics and jewelry, and, in various regions of the Church, even more-strict prohibitions. Today, so I am told, a few of these prohibitions may have been gradually and quietly relaxed.

My dear mother, God rest her soul, left me her Bible, which she read daily. It still has within its well-worn pages religious poems, family pictures of special occasions, and a variety of religious memorabilia that take me back to my youth more than a half century ago. Though my parents knew that I took part, self-consciously and inartfully, in

Saturday night dances at the Ottawa Youth Center, I missed almost all the good movies that came to town, including some distinctly wholesome Disney cartoons and travelogues, and, according to a promise made to my mother sixty or more years ago, I have yet to smoke my first cigarette. Because most of my Ottawa classmates had their own religious practices—Kay Shaughnessy, Mary Alice Harrison, and a small handful of other Catholic kids ate fish on Friday in those days—no one thought much of my religious beliefs and I don't remember being teased or ridiculed about them. Indeed, we helped each other. On Saturday nights in high school I was the designated driver because I didn't drink beer.

A farmer and rancher, outdoorsman, hunter, and fisherman, Dad was a bit more relaxed about these things, though the whole family dutifully attended church at Seventh and Elm Streets Sunday morning and evening and prayer meeting on Wednesdays. Though less inclined by nature to sainthood than my mother, Dad was a true Christian nonetheless. I rarely if ever heard him say a bad thing about anyone else and never knew him to twist the truth or perform a hurtful act. They both set high standards, in their conduct even more than their instructions, and whatever decent qualities I might possess today were the direct result of growing up under their guidance. Because they had to go to work early in life, neither of them graduated from high school. They were both from large families— I had twenty-one aunts and uncles—and they had to work all their lives. My parents were honest, decent, God-fearing people, and I tried my best to live up to their expectations.

My mother had in mind, at least for some time, that I would be a minister. With her encouragement I preached the first of a number of sermons in the Nazarene church when I was eleven years old. My text was from the book of Matthew:

"Where your treasure is, there will your heart be also."
Though by no means a precocious Billy Graham in the making, I somehow carried it off. The small congregation
seemed both amused and, as I recall many years later, a bit
stunned. But, as a vocation, it was not to be. I never felt anything like a calling, and by the time I got to Bethany
Nazarene College I was looking for an alternative form of
service. Indoctrination week of my freshman year that alternative appeared in the form of Professor Prescott Johnson,
teacher of philosophy. Indeed, Professor Johnson was not
only the resident philosopher, he *was* the entire philosophy
department. He gave me little choice but to adopt a philosophy major and, from that, very soon to prepare for a lifetime
of teaching philosophy and religion.

Upon graduation from college, uncanny luck and circumstance got me admitted to the Yale Divinity School,
where I intended to pursue a doctorate in religious and
philosophical studies. As a "fieldwork" requirement during
this period, I was assistant to the minister of a local
Methodist church. Very soon,
however, the realization that I
was pursuing this course
more in an effort to save my
own soul than to qualify for a
profession caused me to start
casting about for some other
direction. About this time
John Kennedy emerged as a
national figure with his challenge, especially to young people, to "ask what you can do for your country."

> Like Samuel Johnson, I came to believe that, "It is our first duty to serve society and, after we have done that, we may attend wholly to the salvation of our own souls."

I joined other students in leafleting around New Haven
on his behalf and gradually came to realize that my instinct
for service could be carried out in the public arena just as

well as, if not better than, in the religious arena. Like Samuel Johnson, I came to believe that, "It is our first duty to serve society and, after we have done that, we may attend wholly to the salvation of our own souls." But it did not occur to me to enter public service as a means of imposing my religious beliefs on others.

It is instructive to recall the hubbub caused by Kennedy's own religious ordeal given the often-feverish nature of our present religious revival. Conservative Protestant ministers, including some leaders in the Nazarene Church, took to their pulpits to decry the dangerous insertion of religion, in this case in the form of John Kennedy's highly suspect Catholicism, into the political arena. In retrospect, there is considerable irony here. For myself, the immediate effect of the Kennedy campaign was to cause me to transfer from the Divinity School and a career in teaching to the Yale Law School and what turned out to be a topsy-turvy career of public service in government and politics.

As my reading and study swiftly turned from the Bible to the U.S. Constitution, Matthew, Mark, Luke, and John were replaced by Thomas, James, John, and Alexander—Jefferson, Madison, Adams, and Hamilton. Writers and thinkers such as Tolstoy and Kierkegaard in some peculiar ways helped me to bridge the gap. Once in law school, I felt much more a sense that I was where I was supposed to be. But I continued to be predominantly motivated by a powerful sense of public service even more than a commitment to the legal profession.

This biographical excursion is worthwhile only to provide qualification to insert myself into the current hothouse debate over religion and politics. There are a number of people with some background in the two fields of religion and politics. There are not that many people with deep personal and family roots in evangelical Protestantism and more than a third of a century of experience in government service, elective office, and public life. Under these circumstances, and given the current politicization of faith or the evangelizing of politics, it seems something of a duty to offer observations, thoughts, and comments in an effort to separate the theological wheat from the political chaff, identify what is socially serious from what is politically motivated, and to try to stake out the common ground for the common good.

One starting place might be the distinctive views of two men, John Wesley and Thomas Jefferson. John Wesley, together with his hymn-writing brother, Charles, was a powerful force in establishing the evangelical and social gospel aspects of eighteenth-century Methodism. The Wesleys, together with George Whitefield and others like them, helped create evangelical Methodism as a movement distinct from the established Church of England. They believed that the eighteenth-century Church of England had become an instrument of social and political elites, a branch of both the British government and British upper classes. They were field preachers; that is to say they took their preaching to ordinary people outside the confines of church walls and rituals. They particularly preached against the neglect of the poor and forgotten. Their revival was as much social as it was religious. They not only preached, they acted. They created training centers for unemployed or abandoned women. They created early versions of today's shelters and soup kitchens. They put their beliefs into actual practice and shamed the neglectful British government. They carried their revival to America and preached against the sin and injustice of slavery in the early American republic. Most important, however, John Wesley did not try to make the

British or American governments the instruments of Methodism or force his doctrines or beliefs on others through the official instruments of government. Nor did he seek government money for his causes by arguing for "faith-based initiatives" or "a thousand points of light." By exposing the rank injustices and inhumanity in supposedly enlightened societies, he sought to change the hearts and souls of men and women, in government and in society, and thereby change their behavior toward those left behind and left out.

When the Church of the Nazarene broke from Methodism, as Methodism had earlier broken from the Church of England, it focused on sin and personal salvation. But there was still a lingering patina of the Wesleyan social gospel sufficient to inspire a young Kansas boy whose instincts were in any case more outward toward public service than inward toward the finer points of why movies were sinful and the new invention of television was not. Indeed, the Wesleyan gospel provided a bridge from religious service to public and social service. Might one not fulfill the teachings of Jesus better by serving others and seeking a more just society than by scrupulous introspection over narrow behavioral doctrines and observance of church law?

While Wesley was preaching the social gospel on both sides of the Atlantic, Thomas Jefferson was preaching the restoration of the republic. That is to say, Jefferson had an ideal of something like the Greek city-state on the new continent, an ideal embodying civic virtue, popular sovereignty, resistance to corruption, and a sense of the commonwealth. It might seem a stretch between Wesley and Jefferson for some, but in its pure form civic virtue is not too far from the gospel of social justice, avoidance of sin not too far from resistance to corruption, and service to others not too different from a sense of the commonwealth. At least it did not seem so to me in the 1960s, and it does not seem so today in the twenty-first century.

As Wesley did not seek to convert the political structures of his day to Methodism, he also did not seek to have Methodism usurp eighteenth-century British politics. He would have been among the first to appreciate Jefferson's insistence on the separation of church and state and the dangers of trying to mingle the two. It was one thing, for Wesley, to place social injustice on the public stage and cry for action. It was quite another to seek to make church doctrine official public policy. In my own transition from scholar of religion to public servant, the Wesleyan social gospel played a crucial role, and it remains a powerful motivating force for me even today.

All this recitation of my own background is merely to qualify myself to comment on the motivations and energies of the current religious revival, particularly where it seeks to place itself at the service of partisan politics. An important first step in this effort is to explore what people, especially politicians, mean when they talk about faith and values and to draw distinctions between doctrines concerning "the culture of life," "faith-based initiatives," rewards for wealth, and the "saved" as a privileged class, on the one hand, and the ideal of social justice, ladders of opportunity, income distribution, and care for the "damned," on the other hand.

> Any serious effort to place "faith" and "values" at the center of current politics must not only be more explicit about "faith" in what and "values" selected by whom, it must also itself perform according to the high standards it seeks to set for others.

Any serious effort to place "faith" and "values" at the center of current politics must not only be more explicit about "faith" in what and "values" selected by whom, it must also itself perform according to the high standards it seeks to set for others. Risks of hypocrisy are in direct proportion to claims for purity.

A "culture of life" as applied to preservation of a fetus or a brain-dead patient fails both as a moral standard and a political objective when it is not also applied to prisoners on death row and to civilian casualties in mistaken invasions. Faith-based initiatives and a thousand points of light fail as public policy when they are demonstrably insufficient to remedy the plight of one in five American children in poverty and millions of homeless and unemployed families. This is even more true when public money is sought for religious organizations, probably in violation of the Constitution, while public funds for public programs designed to help those children and those families are being denied. Tax cuts for the wealthy and powerful, especially in the face of deficits left as legacies to future generations, are not part of any "faith" that can be reconciled with Jesus' admonition that it would be harder for a rich man to enter the kingdom of God than for a camel to pass through the eye of a needle.

These observations require consideration at greater length, but they suffice here as warning to those who would easily preach a political agenda based on some vague "faith" without the moral and spiritual content, consistency, and practical performance to back it up. Politicians who seek support in religious communities by endorsing their agendas need be careful both about the internal consistency of those agendas and their own consistency in carrying out the true faith upon which they claim to act. The gospel of Jesus, encompassing as it does the laws of Moses, is exacting, and it is not subject to convenient selection. Life means life, all life. Charity means charity, public and "faith based." Love means love, not just for one's wealthy allies and powerful friends, but also toward those who hate you. Peace means peace, not the pursuit of warlike goals based on flawed justifications. Those who seek to create a "faith-based" government and insert "values," however ill-defined, into their political platforms should proceed both with utmost caution against the slippery descent into hypocrisy and with utmost humility given the purity of the standards which the founders of those faiths established for those who claim to believe in them.

Faith in What?

By its very nature, politics lends itself to generalization. Terms and phrases that are freighted with meaning can be used by political figures in ways that suggest concurrence with any and all who care about those words but have their own meaning for them. "Faith" is a classic example. When used in the context of "faith-based initiative" it means whatever the hearer wants it to mean. To most Christians it would mean an activity carried out by a church or seminary. Presumably Jews would hear it to mean an activity carried out by a synagogue. And to Muslims it would be heard to mean community outreach by a mosque.

Used in this way, "faith" is a synonym for "religious." Why not then simply say "religious initiatives" instead of "faith based"? Who knows? Clever politicians perhaps are sensitive to the First Amendment separation of church and state and its prohibition against laws related to the establishment of religion. Besides which, if you use the word "religion," there is still the problem of *which* religion. The current religious-political revival embraces those who declare that America was founded as a Christian nation and ought to officially confirm this fact at every point. They do not seem particularly interested in promoting religion generally.

Whatever the reason for remaining purposely obscure about "faith" in what—and the creators of this new language are not saying—the early twenty-first-century religious revival as imposed upon politics relies strongly on the language of "faith" and "values." Shouldn't we know, shouldn't we discuss what these terms mean? Shouldn't those who use these terms be required to tell us exactly what they are saying when they use these words? Clearly they convey a set of meanings to those who support the politicians who use them. They represent a kind of code, what today's pundits call "buzzwords," to those who speak this language.

Indeed, coded political communications require rather cynical use of special language, including "dog whistle" messages. As the phrase suggests, these are communications sent on a frequency only the select can hear. If your ears are not keen enough to be tuned to the secret frequency, you will not be able to get the message. These kinds of communications are meant to shut out those who are not among the elect. The need for this kind of code language in a democracy raises all kinds of questions and suspicions.

As one brought up in the evangelical Protestant tradition and educated in an old-line, traditional seminary, faith means belief in Jesus as the Christ as the savior of the world, as the redeemer of sinners, being all mankind, and it means acceptance of an explicit creedal doctrine. How one defines faith for other religions is a separate undertaking and best left to those steeped in those religions. The principal question for us here is, What does President George W. Bush, and any one of a number of other political officials who use these terms, mean when they use them *in a political context*? Do they mean faith in an explicitly Christian context and, if so, in the Protestant tradition or in the Catholic tradition? Because there are very important doctrinal differences between them. And if it is faith in the Protestant tradition, which of the hundreds of offshoots of Protestantism? Or do they intend it to include anyone who is affiliated, nominally or otherwise, with any kind of religious heritage of which there are thousands, some being rather bizarre (to put it politely)?

To raise these questions is not to be tendentious. Heavily value-laden language should be used very carefully when employed for political purposes, especially in a nation founded on the idea of keeping religion separate from government. Obviously, in an age of religious revival there is every temptation for politicians to try to identify with the concerns of the revivalists as a means of seeking support: "I'll support your religious efforts if you support my political ones. Better yet, let's merge the two and make it simple."

But this approach, presuming it is not totally cynical, is fraught with monumental peril, both for its threat to constitutional guarantees against any form of official religion and for the inevitable political divisions it promises between those who choose to place themselves in the "faith" camp, however they choose to define it, and those who do not. The same dangers apply to the popular and even more casual use of the all-purpose term "values." What values? Whose values? Who gets to choose the values that are in official favor with the government currently in power? Like defining the terms of a debate, he who gets to choose the values dominates the political discussion. For anyone preaching the politics of "values," there should be a requirement to specify exactly what values we are talking about, and some means must be found for determining the authority of those self-selected to choose those values.

Clearly there are a set of ideals and principles, values if you will, embodied in historical American culture and society. This is not an argument against values. It is an argument against the use of terms such as "values" in such a purposely vague way so that they represent a secret code language that only the select elites or political insiders can understand and communicate. The values—I prefer ideals and principles—at the core of my philosophy as a human being and an American are justice, fairness, courage, honor, integrity, duty, idealism, and compassion. Politically they also include commitment to constitutional democracy and the principles of the republic. Though it is not clear, since those who use the "values" code words do not define them, I somehow doubt that these are exactly the values they have in mind.

To question exactly what "faith" and "values" mean is, to those who use these vague terms, to engage in the evil of relativism, that is to suggest that these terms have no absolute truth or meaning but are up to the individual to define. But by purposefully choosing not to define what they mean by this language, it is those who adopt these terms who invite relativism. Or, as I believe, it is to leave words freighted with meaning undefined so that everyone at large can believe they include *their* faith and *their* values, while all the while the political and religious insiders know exactly, in very precise ways, what these terms communicate. If this is what they are up to, this is an extremely clever device to have it both ways: we faith and values people stand for all faiths and all values, but among ourselves we mean fundamentalist Protestant faith (including apocalyptic separation of us from all those sinners who have adopted other faiths) and specially defined conservative political and social values.

> This is not an argument against values. It is an argument against the use of terms such as "values" in such a purposely vague way so that they represent a secret code language that only the select elites or political insiders can understand and communicate.

This all works out politically and conveniently so that

there are "faith" candidates and parties and "non-faith" parties and candidates. Curiously, the former almost always seem to be conservative members of one political party. This merging of evangelical Protestant faith and neo-conservative partisan politics has taken place only in the last fifteen or so years, not a very long time. And, in its more honest forms, it is becoming more straightforward and less clandestine. In the most recent presidential election, evangelical ministers publicly urged their church members to vote for George W. Bush and conservative candidates largely of one party. The same First Amendment that prohibits official religion also protects free speech.

It is far more preferable, it seems to me, for religious leaders to be open and honest about their political activism than to have it hinted at in code words, winks, and nudges. Nevertheless, the excommunication of members of at least one Baptist church for not voting for George W. Bush, as instructed by their pastor, dramatically illustrates the dangers of intermingling religion and politics.

The matter for concern is less about religious organizations supporting political candidates and more about religious organizations supporting political candidates who will actively and aggressively seek to impose the religious agenda of those organizations on the rest of the country through appointments to high administrative office, through the judiciary, and through congressional legislation. For their support, the religious organizations, largely fundamentalist Protestant or conservative Catholic, now demand the right to screen candidates for political and judicial appointment. During the current administration, it is virtually inconceivable that anyone who is at odds with the religious right will reach the federal bench or high administration position. That behind-the-scenes religious screening process excludes a huge number of highly qualified Americans who would serve their country honorably and well.

This narrowing of the gate of admission to public service also occurs at a time in our history when the U.S. Commission on National Security/21st Century, which I cochaired, found that our national security was endangered because of the declining caliber and quality of citizens entering all forms of public service. There is a trade-off. We may get cabinet and subcabinet officers and federal judges who pass muster on the "faith and values" score but who are demonstrably less qualified to carry out their constitutional duties, promote fairness and justice for all, and defend the security of the United States. The recent history of administrative and judicial appointments seems to bear out this conclusion with a vengeance. Simply because you pass restrictive religious and ideological tests does not necessarily qualify you to run the country.

There is a strong suggestion concerning those who choose not to adopt the vague values rhetoric that they are value-less, that they do not have values, that they may even be anti-values. It is should not seem surprising that, politically, those not expounding the "values" language, whether from confusion, disagreement, or disgust, are often those extravagantly loathed "liberals." There is an almost inevitable logic. The plight in which the country finds itself is the product of losing our values; liberals have created all mischief; therefore, liberals have no values. Therefore, to regain our unspecified values, we must get rid of all the liberals. Closed systems have their own unassailable internal logic. Unfortunately, closed systems quickly become intellectually totalitarian.

Such closed systems—religious, political, and intellectual—are based on absolute certainty. The current closed system engineered by the merger of the religious right and neo-conservatism is no exception. Its certainties are these: there are the saved and the damned, and we are the saved; wealth is a product of virtue and therefore deserves further reward; America's destiny is to slay foreign demons; even if we are the minority, it is our duty to impose our beliefs on the majority; the wretched among us deserve private charity but not public assistance; international alliances are useless at best and perfidious at worst because we are peerless; and we see things more clearly than you do because we rule by divine right.

Lacking these insights and certainties, and subject to occasional doubts and uncertainties, those of us not in the closed system are pilloried as weak, adrift, and lacking in the moral fiber required for leadership. But the qualities of this closed, doctrinaire, and rigid system, under the unwavering glare of sunlight look more like arrogance, smugness, elitism, superiority, and self-satisfaction. These characteristics might be used to describe a certain type of tycoon, corporate buccaneer, or overbearing academic, but they most certainly do not characterize Jesus. The founder of the Christian religion and the object of the true Christian faith drove the money changers from the temple, castigated the smug Pharisees ("blind leaders of the blind"), preached about the obstacles between the rich man and the kingdom of heaven, selected his disciples from the ranks of the working poor, routinely supped with ordinary people, ministered to the poor and insisted that others do likewise, forgave sinners, and told those around him not to judge others lest they themselves be judged.

Jesus challenged conventional wisdom and closed systems founded on exclusivity and smug certainties. Those who genuinely have faith in him share in his blessing of the

peacemakers, they who hunger and thirst after righteousness, the poor in spirit, they who mourn, the merciful, and
the pure in heart. Those who claim to believe in "values"
would do well to read the Sermon on the Mount. There are
values. The difficulty is not in imposing them on others but
in living up to them ourselves.

I read nothing in the Sermon on the Mount about taking
over political parties, selecting ideological judges, dominating
the legislative process, seeking ways around campaign finance
laws, or casually demonizing your opponents. If today's
pious politicians seriously cared about faith and values, they
would seek to take on the qualities of Jesus: humility,
understanding, compassion, tolerance, forgiveness, and sor-
row for the miseries of the world. If these qualities describe anyone today preaching
"values" and "faith" in the political arena, his or her name
does not readily come to mind.

> **If today's pious politicians seriously cared about faith and values, they would seek to take on the qualities of Jesus: humility, understanding, compassion, tolerance, forgiveness, and sorrow for the miseries of the world.**

Not only are those seeking to impose their narrow
interpretation of the Christian religion on the realm of public policy obliged to live up to and espouse the complete
teachings of Jesus, they are also obliged to acknowledge the
unique freedom and independence guaranteed to all
Americans under our Constitution. Taken from early revolutionary America, the New Hampshire state slogan, "Don't
Tread on Me," encapsulates a truth at the heart of America's
polity: do not try to impose your beliefs on others. You may
preach, you may argue, you may speak, rally, organize, advo-
cate, and you may seek to convert your fellow citizen, but do

not attempt, by law or regulation, to force another American to adopt your religious beliefs.

It is a far cry from "Congress shall make no laws concerning the establishment of religion" to "Congress shall adopt my religious beliefs and make them the law of the land."

The Tyranny of the Faithful: The Dangers of Theocracy

Early 2005 found the United States government, especially the United States Senate, deadlocked over the confirmation of a small number of presidential nominees for the federal court of appeals. Described by the administration and their proponents as "people of faith," some of these nominees not only made clear their support for reconsideration and probably reversal of abortion rights, they also demonstrated a judicial temperament adverse to the rights of workers, environmental regulations, corporate accountability, and a variety of policies dating to the age of the New Deal. Their opponents, largely members of the more liberal party in the Senate and a number of civic and social organizations, argued that these nominees were identifiably outside even the most charitable definition of the mainstream of national political opinion. That is to say, they were well beyond even traditional conservatism.

In the debate it was also pointed out that opposition by very conservative forces in the Senate and the nation had successfully blocked at least this number of federal judges nominated by previous administrations but deemed too liberal by their opponents. And, it was argued, the vast majority of recent appointments, well above 90 percent and including some very conservative nominees, had been approved by the Senate. Only at the very last moment did a coalition of moderate senators, more concerned with the unique character of the Senate as a deliberative body than satisfaction of an ideological agenda, manage for the time being to salvage Senate procedures protecting the rights of the minority. But the struggle has only just begun.

This struggle between the religious right and neo-conservatism, on the one hand, and liberal and traditional mainstream forces, on the other, eventuated from the refusal of a number of federal courts to uphold legislation enacted to codify a specifically religious agenda or to overrule lower court decisions rejecting elements of that agenda. Thus the conclusion was reached that achieving the longed-for religious revival in the political sphere meant not just putting a favorable president in the White House and electing a majority of conservative, pro-revival members to both houses of Congress, it finally required appointment of judges across the spectrum of the federal judiciary who were in agreement with an agenda of revivalist values and beliefs, pre–New Deal, devil-take-the-hindmost social principles, and radical, blunt-force economics.

The full agenda of religious right "values," laissez-faire economics, antigovernment biases, neo-conservative foreign policies, and rightist orthodoxy, requires a judiciary compliant with it. It does no good to convert a Jeffersonian public school system into private parochial schools, to make churches the instruments of the state by transferring public funds from social programs to them, to pass laws restricting reproductive rights, to expand law enforcement's intrusive reach in the name of security, or to torture or indefinitely detain terror suspects if a judge or court from the pre-revivalist past overturns those actions on constitutional grounds. The full religious revolution cannot be realized without a federal judiciary, up to and including at least five members of the Supreme Court, that shares those ideals and goals.

The New American Theocracy requires judges who will go along and who will continue going along for the remainder of their lives. The ultimate goal is a Supreme Court philosophically attuned to the principles and purposes of those seeking a state that incorporates and promotes their religious beliefs. Only then will the presidential decrees and compliant congressional actions sought by the right be safe from assault by a judiciary dedicated to the proposition that the law is established within the framework of the United States Constitution, not the Bible.

The new theocrats do not know and do not seem to want to know that judges take an oath of office requiring them to uphold the Constitution. The fact that they may (or may not) place their hand upon a Bible and swear, "so help me, God" in taking that oath does not in any way mean that they are to place their, or anyone else's, theological doctrines above those principles spelled out in the Constitution and laws of the United States.

But does not democracy require that the majority prevail, that the will of the majority is to determine the direction of the nation? And did not the majority of Americans elect a president and a Congress committed to the agenda of those dedicated to a theocratic democracy? It is too much to assume that a majority of those who voted for George W. Bush for president or for any individual senator or house member were of the same mind on the very wide variety of religious and social issues promoted by the religious right. It is clear that the religious right has established a dominant position within one political party, a position that permits it to impose its veto on candidates for office, proposed legislation, and judicial appointments. But this position does not make it a majority even in one political party, let alone in the nation. A somewhat similar position was occupied by the organized labor movement in the Democratic Party up until recently. But that did not mean that a majority of Democrats were members of that movement or even that they agreed with the labor movement on all issues.

It is one thing to be one member of a coalition that makes up one political party and it is quite another to assume a minority position in one party that requires that party, all institutions of government, and the nation at large to accept the religious doctrines of that minority. The religious right in America, empowered by compliant elected officials, some of whom are intimidated by that element, is seeking a dictatorship of the minority. There are more than a few authoritarian and totalitarian examples in the world where this has taken place, but not in a constitutional democracy such as the United States.

One can only wonder at the response of a Jefferson or a Madison to such an effort.

To resist the tyranny of the minority and its efforts to create a religious republic is not to deny the rights and privileges of those with deep religious convictions to participate in the democratic processes. In an age of only casual citizen interest in the politics of our nation, all who care about our country and its future are to be welcomed into the systems of governance that affect our lives. All should be welcome to express their views and to attempt to persuade others toward them. But simply because we are a democracy and all have a right to be heard does not suggest that those who speak the loudest, the longest, and the most intensely thereby gain greater credibility or authority for their points of view. Those religious revivalists newly engaged in political activities seem to believe that they gain special credence simply because of the sheer intensity of their beliefs: "I really care strongly about this so I demand that you accept my position."

Anyone making these arguments invites the inevitable response that he or she is the enemy of religion and those who avow religious belief. Such is not the case. Though failing often, I seek to live my deeply felt religious convictions every day of my life. More than any other factor, my decision to seek public office, to be involved in political campaigns, to support candidates, to promote public policies, and to innovate with new ideas all come from a profound desire to improve the nation, the world in which I live, and the world my children will inherit. And that desire is the direct product of my religious training and upbringing. I yield to no one, including the most dedicated, vociferous, and intense proponent of religion in politics, in my effort to translate my faith into action.

> Those on the right seem to think that they deserve a special place on the public platform simply because they are intense in their beliefs and that their intensity is somehow significantly more spiritual than anyone else's.

But personal faith must be translated into the political context not politics translated into the religious context.

Those on the right seem to think that they deserve a special place on the public platform simply because they are intense in their beliefs and that their intensity is somehow significantly more spiritual than anyone else's. But I hold to my religious beliefs and am as committed to the liberal humanitarian agenda they command in me, every bit as strongly as any person on the religious right. It does not seem to occur to those on the religious right that another person's spiritual beliefs might lead them to different political conclusions, conclusions that we should care for the poor, seek peaceful resolution of conflict before making war, act as nature's stewards, or be committed to social justice. The religious right is entitled to its interpretation of religious truth. It is *not* entitled to conclude that the intensity of its passions grants it a position of political superiority.

There is a huge and insurmountable difference between these two approaches. I do not seek to force others to accept my religious beliefs. My religious beliefs cause me to want to improve the lives of others. I do not seek to wage an imperial crusade in the Middle East or elsewhere, especially where our interests and motives are complicated by factors such as our heavy dependence on foreign oil. My religious beliefs cause me to want to find peaceful ways—even while crushing terrorists by force where necessary—to offer democratic freedom, market opportunity, and intercultural and religious exchange and goodwill to those in the Middle East and elsewhere who deserve a better chance.

Living one's beliefs in everyday life and seeking to influence by example and contribution is one thing. Imposing one's beliefs on others by political manipulation and coercion is quite another. The great danger in the politicization of the early twenty-first-century religious revival, or the religious occupation of politics, is the corruption of both politics and religion. Organized religion that seeks to occupy political power loses its purity and its purpose. Jesus sought to change people's hearts, not their political parties. He did not try to overthrow the Roman Empire. He did seek to transform the lives of those who were subject to the Roman Empire. When any faith becomes an instrument of politics, it no longer is a religious faith. It is simply a political instrument like all others. And that is the way it is being used today.

Likewise, when a political party tries to make the church part of its coalition, it confuses its secular purposes with the church's eternal mission. No political party or institution is pure enough or good enough to make itself an instrument of religion. Its only purpose is an earthly one, to govern and to govern well. Political institutions have no right or capability to sort through religious truth and determine which to accept and which to reject. If twenty-first-century Americans try to join the church to politics they will do nothing but restore the frightful age of medieval Europe. Popes will be selecting kings and kings will be dethroning popes. Only murderous mayhem can ensue, and only some future Machiavelli will know how to advise the prince to manipulate the church to ensure his own power.

> No political party or institution is pure enough or good enough to make itself an instrument of religion. Its only purpose is an earthly one, to govern and to govern well.

Americans have always demonstrated skepticism and occasional apprehension toward true believers, those who presume to own the truth. It is one thing to have deep convictions. It is something else to believe that only you are right and that it is your duty to impose your convictions on all the rest. The separation between conviction and fanaticism is thinner than most would suppose: it is a very short step from righteous belief to the mentality of the crusader. Today in America the religious centrifuge is whirling ever faster in melding revivalism, fundamentalism, and a foreign policy dedicated to imperialism. If one has a divine mission to convert the unbeliever in America to a true doctrinal path, then that mission must surely extend to the unbeliever abroad.

The logic is as follows: nineteen fanatical Muslim terrorists attacked America and killed more than 3,000 of our citizens; they came from a region rife with fanatics and terrorists; we will always be subject to attack from that region so long as it is left to its own devices; therefore, we have no choice but to impose our will upon the region. (Besides, a great deal of our oil, oil vital to our profligate lifestyle, is under that region's sand.) There is little question that those most concerned with reconstituting American politics along religious lines were on the forefront of those supporting Gulf War II. They presumably will be equally supportive of Gulf Wars III, IV, and so on.

Occupation of the Middle East offers the opportunity for exportation of democracy, capitalism, and quite possibly the Christian faith. All are belief systems freely available for exportation. The devil is not in the exportation, but rather in the occupation it supposes. To the degree that occupation becomes permanent, it is an act of empire. And America, with the possible exception of the Spanish-American War era, has not been nor has it sought to be an imperial power. President James Monroe declared our hemisphere off-limits to European colonization while steadfastly asserting that the United States had no imperial interests of its own. His secretary of state, John Quincy Adams, famously asserted that, "We go not abroad seeking demons to destroy." We may try to export democracy, capitalism, and the Christian faith, but it would be a very great danger to America's character to become an imperial power as a means of doing so.

As it is a great danger to constitutional democracy for America to become a theocracy, so is it an even greater danger to our republican heritage for America to become a theocratic empire. Either one, and certainly both together, would fundamentally change the nature of our nation and our society. Domination of American politics by a religious minority and domination of American foreign policy by that minority are twin dangers.

Were we to become a theocratic empire, then will the

First Amendment protection of church from state and state from church be abandoned as obsolete. Then will crusaders mount their steeds and ride off to save the world from its many infidels. Then will the church be running the schools using public funds to do so. Then will the ministers and priests and pastors be conveying the government's latest policies from their pulpits and platforms. Then will judges be confirmed only after they have been successfully approved by deacons. Then will political candidates raise campaign funds in places of worship.

On reflection, perhaps we are already there.

America as Avenging Angel

With the rise of evangelical fervor and the political-religious right, a new approach to American foreign policy has thus emerged. It is unilateral, sometimes dictatorial, and occasionally apocalyptic. It would seem that we might appoint the mad abolitionist John Brown as secretary of state. Most important is the fact that this new foreign policy has about it a certain smell of empire.

The fact that the United States of America was founded 218 years ago as a republic seems not to matter to those fashioning the new foreign policy. The neo-conservative project to position the United States as the world's dominant power and to use that power to preside over entire regions such as the Middle East has been strongly endorsed by those who seek also to infuse domestic policy with religious doctrine.

A careful review of President George W. Bush's statements and those of his administration up to the declaration of victory in Iraq yields little evidence of the true purpose of America's invasion. The world is now familiar with the arguments: Iraq possesses weapons of mass destruction and "we know where they are"; Iraq has or will soon have "nuclear capability"; Iraq harbors and supports terrorists planning attacks on the United States; Iraq itself is a threat to U.S. national security. All have proved untrue and are no longer offered as justification for the United States' preventive war on Iraq, an action with precedent in United States history possibly only in our occupation of the Philippines more than a century ago.

Today the administration offers the rationalization that deposing Saddam Hussein was necessary to achieve peace in the Middle East. This argument was never used in the run-up to war against Iraq for the simple reason that it is an act of empire. Leave aside the fact that the argument is severely flawed, as subsequent history has shown. We are now bogged down in urban warfare against indigenous militias, a style of warfare for which we are largely unprepared and which causes unsustainable levels of civilian casualties. We have substantially contributed to anti-American sentiments throughout the region and possibly throughout the Islamic world.

Costs to the United States taxpayers are already easily exceeding $200 billion (honestly predicted before the war by one Bush economic advisor who was fired for his honesty) with no end in sight. Somewhere between 35,000 and 50,000 civilian Iraqi casualties are also among the costs, though this morally important fact is rarely discussed by the religious right. Much more important to most Americans are the almost 25,000 American combat and noncombat (including psychological) casualties. We don't know the exact number because the Pentagon will not release noncombat casualty figures and the press does not seem capable of finding out. Before the war I predicted that, if the Iraqi Republican Guard chose to fight in the cities, American casualties could mount to between 5,000 and 10,000. General Barry McCaffrey predicted as many as 50,000 American casualties under these circumstances. We were both ridiculed by conservative editorial boards and commentators. Instead of the Republican Guard, we are now faced with a militia insurgency carrying out the same strategy.

Had the international legal standards for preemptive warfare been met, it could plausibly have been argued that America's invasion of Iraq was not imperial in nature. That traditional standard permits preemptive action where a threat is "immediate and unavoidable," a standard clearly not met where Iraq is concerned. So, much else is at work here. It is a fanciful, but not idealistic, notion that the United States can invade and occupy a nation situated in the center of the complex and troubled Middle East, install a favorable democratic government, and use its position as friendly military occupier to condition the behavior of neighboring nations, introduce "democracy," at the point of a bayonet if necessary, and bring Middle Eastern combatants to the bargaining table.

This strategy has at least two fatal flaws. It is an act of empire. And it was never disclosed to the American people so that they, acting in their capacity as popular sovereigns, could ratify it. Those who applaud this strategy argue that America is an empire and ought just to get on with it, and writers such as Robert Kaplan who understand the difficulties of selling imperialism to a republican polity, therefore urge empire by "stealth."

Why should we care one way or the other? The answer is simple. The United States cannot be simultaneously republic and empire. For evidence, see Rome (circa 65 B.C.). We salute the flag of the United States of America "and the Republic for which it stands." Since the Greek city-states, republics have shared certain immutable qualities: civic virtue, or citizen participation; popular sovereignty; resistance to corruption by special interests; and a sense of the common good. Empires consolidate power in the hands of the few, seek expanded influence by force if necessary, export centralized administrations to foreign lands, dictate terms to lesser powers, and manage foreign occupied peoples for their own political and commercial advantage.

Bush administration neo-conservatives claim none of these characteristics for their imperial actions in Iraq. They claim to want only what is best for the Iraqi people. Some Iraqis are resisting, in murderous ways, these benign benefits. Even more to the point, even if one were to concede the best motives to the religious right and the neo-conservatives, the imperial project is not who we are or who we should wish to become. Woodrow Wilson cannot be claimed as a forerunner here, for his project to make the world safe for democracy was benign, not militaristic, and internationalist, not unilateralist. These are huge differences.

> This should be America's twenty-first-century project, restoring our republic, not projecting imperial power into venues we are, by our very nature, unequipped to dominate.

The imperial project is in direct contradiction to America's constitutional principles. We are a republic, not an empire, and we are a republic much in need of restoration, as resistance to corruption and the exercise of civic virtue erode. This should be America's twenty-first-century project, restoring our republic, not projecting imperial power into venues we are, by our very nature, unequipped to dominate.

For some involved in the current American religious revival, this new imperial foreign policy is merely an extension of the effort to remake America along the lines of religious doctrine. It would be difficult, if not impossible, to infuse the political policies and structures of the United States with faith and values only as they apply within our shores. In a world of globalization, a religiously revived America must also be an America that carries the message of that revival around the world. "Go, ye, therefore, into all the world and preach the gospel." But, like too many missionary endeavors throughout history, preaching the gospel can quickly become imposing the gospel, and there is little evidence that Jesus meant this admonition for national governments.

Clearly, America stands for certain principles. I believe those principles represent our greatest power, for they attract the peoples of the world to us in direct proportion to our willingness and ability to live up to those principles. They are the foundation of our constitutional democracy. We believe in free elections, freedom of assembly, and a free press. We believe in equality for all, regardless of race, gender, or circumstance of birth. We believe in a rule of law and equal justice under that law for all. We believe every vote to be equal. We believe in liberty and justice for all. We believe those in the minority have rights that must be protected. We believe in a system of government where power is balanced and checked among its branches. We believe that the church and the state should be separate.

Nowhere in the Constitution, our founding debates, or these principles is there a suggestion that the United States is to be the world's avenging angel. Indeed, John Quincy Adams merely echoed founding principles with his warning against searching for demons to destroy abroad. Our founders saw the republican experiment on the new continent as distinctly different from the monarchy- and church-ridden politics of old Europe, as much as anything because the wars and turmoils of that region intermingled politics and religion. The new republic could not succeed if it imported the vicious religious-dominated politics of the old countries.

Yet, soon after the terrorist attacks of 9/11, President Bush began to describe the world in terms of good and evil. Surely there is both good and evil in the world. But should that fact be the basis of a great nation's foreign policy? There is little in American history to cause us to believe it should.

Is there, perhaps, such a dramatic confrontation between good and evil today, unlike other times in human history, that it should cause us to reorient our dealings with other nations along theological lines? It would be difficult to say so. Are we righteous enough, are we pure enough, to set our-

> Are we righteous enough, are we pure enough, to set ourselves above other nations, including other nations with deep religious heritages, as the moral arbiters of global behavior?

selves above other nations, including other nations with deep religious heritages, as the moral arbiters of global behavior? We may have a ways to go.

Our greatest leaders, among them Abraham Lincoln, have always cautioned us toward humility and asked us to consider that we may be in error in the eyes of God. Humility is a quality now in short supply. To set ourselves up as the world's judge and jury and to play the role of avenging angel for all those we determine to be evildoers is to set the United States on a course it has never before followed, one which requires a degree of moral purity it has yet to earn. Did we believe ourselves to be in the right in World Wars I and II? Of course. Even earlier, did the cause of emancipation and salvation of the union warrant the bloody Civil War? Lincoln himself, with much self-doubt and anguish at the suffering and slaughter, believed it to be so. But, in the process, he always invoked God's mercy and forgiveness. To question America's role as avenging angel is not to suggest that there is not right and wrong, justice and injustice. It is to state, however, that any description of America's purpose in the world based upon theological precepts is a prescription for arrogance, self-righteousness, and hypocrisy.

How, for example, are we to promote a "culture of life" around the world when we are one of the very few nations, and possibly the only democracy, to still impose the death sentence? Among the others is North Korea, a founding member of the "axis of evil." In 2004, 94 percent of all executions in the world were carried out by just four countries: China, Iran, Vietnam, and the United States. (If Americans find themselves uncomfortable in the company of two of the last communist nations on Earth and the largest theocracy in the Middle East, also a member of the "axis of evil," it would be understandable.) How can we raise up the standard of the rule of law when hundreds of "detainees" are denied even minimal due process of law and are endlessly imprisoned incognito, and sometimes tortured, without charges? If our cause is righteous and our purpose just, why are we not told the number of civilian casualties in Iraq, the total number of combat and noncombat American casualties, or even permitted to see pictures of American coffins coming home?

The role of Old Testament judge was a demanding one. It not only required sobriety and wisdom, it also required absolute integrity in thought and deed, maximum obedience to the law, and uprightness in all dealings with fellow men. Even then, few were chosen as instruments of the wrath of God. "Vengeance is mine, sayeth the Lord," simply because mortal humans could never achieve the degree of moral perfection required to render His vengeance on each other. The United States may have achieved a relatively higher plane of constitutional democracy than any republic in history, but that is still a far reach to the degree of perfection required to dispense God's judgment, God's wrath, or God's vengeance.

Jesus cautioned against judging one another for the same reason. He did not, of course, mean on the legal plane. He insisted that his followers obey the laws of Moses and of man and to suffer the consequences if they did not. Jesus did not claim to have come to overthrow the judicial system of the Jewish society in which he was born and of which he was a member. He was cautioning his followers against judgments involving the human heart. For we cannot know either what evil lurks or what good abides there. Sinfulness is an infinitely more complex matter than simple obedience to the law. What politician can set himself or herself up as moral judge? Who can possibly know all the complexities at work in another person's life?

Do nations violate international law and endanger others? Of course. If that behavior endangers the security of another nation is there just cause for action, including military action, to reduce or eliminate that threat? Of course. But these rules are well established and do not require any nation, including ours, undertaking to divide the world between good and evil as the basis for conducting its relations. During World War II we made common cause with Stalin and Soviet Russia. During the Cold War we found it expedient to support a variety of dictators, oligarchs, and even assassins to contain the perceived communist threat. The "lesser evil" theory has often guided American foreign policy and will undoubtedly continue to. But a principled foreign policy does not have to choose between the lesser good or the lesser evil.

As dangerous as it would be for the United States to behave as an imperial power in the Middle East or elsewhere, it would be even more dangerous for us to become a religious empire, a nation of crusaders. Part of the deep anger and hostility to the United States in the Arab world is based on the suspicion that our two wars in the region (so far) are all about oil, but even more that, to protect oil supplies or for many other reasons, we intend to impose both our political will and *our cultural and religious values* on that region. We are late entries into a region where all roads lead to Jerusalem, a city not only at the crossroads of three major religions but one whose history is revealed in the layered excavations of ages of tyrants, despots, crusaders, and occupying powers. It is useless to speculate whether it might have made a difference if even one person in the White House or Pentagon had read the history of the British occupation of Iraq before we decided to march on Baghdad.

"Pride goeth before the fall," say the Scriptures. And pride where nations are concerned takes the form of hubris, the sense that one is so favored by heaven that anything is possible and all can be achieved. The hubris of America's avenging angel crusade against evil has its roots in the end of the Cold War and the collapse of any political, economic, or military rival in the world. If the Taliban government in Afghanistan deserved to fall, as it did, for harboring al Qaeda during its attacks on the United States, then why did not Saddam Hussein also deserve to fall simply because he had come to be seen as a troublemaker in the troubled Middle East? We were simply preempting him before he attacked us. Now that it is clear that he had neither the capability nor intent to attack us, his overthrow became preventive instead of preemptive. And if Saddam Hussein can be prevented from ever again being a possible threat to us, why not employ the doctrine of preventive war against any number of other nations? Leaving aside the fact that there is nothing in American constitutional history, let alone religious teachings, to justify such actions and the fact that there are practical limits on the numbers of times the troops of even the mightiest military power can be sent into battle, such a policy of preventive warfare assumes to a stunning degree the righteousness and moral superiority of the United States. To determine on one's own what states deserve to live and what states deserve to die is breathtaking in its audacity, arrogance, and hubris. But if prevention is justified in Iraq, who will decide where it is not justified?

America as Avenging Angel is not an America I can recognize. Nor is it an America any of our founders could recognize. We may debate, and should, the degree to which religious belief should shape the laws and government of the United States. But there should be no debate in favor of the proposition that America has been divinely selected to govern the world according to the religious predispositions of a minority of its citizens.

Too many on the right have confused faith with doctrine. For, as someone once said, "A faith is something you die for. A doctrine is something you kill for."

Perhaps the day will come when we are pure enough, righteous enough, and worthy enough to deserve the blessing of the Almighty to conquer the Earth in the name of the cross. We should not expect that day to occur anytime soon.

The Awful Warmth of the Gospel of Jesus

There are many truths concerning the teachings of Jesus, but one is central: his teachings must be taken whole. Throughout the past 2,000 years, one demagogue or another has selected a particular parable or saying to justify almost any kind of behavior. And Christians throughout the ages have also found it convenient to place passages from the Old Testament, particularly where wrath and judgment were concerned, in Jesus' mouth. But our concern here is with the application of religion, at this particular time a revival of fundamentalist Protestant religion, to conservative American politics. The question that must be answered is whether the religious teachings being incorporated into today's conservative politics accurately reflect the views of Christianity's original founder. In other words, is the political-religious right telling the whole story?

Christian fundamentalism is not much different from fundamentalism in other religions. It stresses strict behavior, strict attendance at worship, inflexible codes of conduct, adherence to established doctrine, and acceptance of priestly authority. Emphasis is placed on conformity to traditional norms and acceptance of traditional values. Tradition in this context may represent only thirty or forty years. Fundamentalism sees the world in blacks and whites, not grays and plaids, in clear categories of good and evil, and in sharp divisions between believers and nonbelievers. In such a starkly contrasting world, fundamentalism is necessarily judgmental. Perhaps above all else, fundamentalism is self-certain and self-assured. To doubt or to question is to err. I know about this from personal experience.

To find justification for its political agenda in the early twenty-first century and for its efforts to dictate terms to a complex democracy, the religious right must look elsewhere than to the gospel of Jesus. The hallmarks of the religious right are fundamentalism, strict adherence to religious law and doctrine, focus on sin and moral error, exclusion, and judgmentalism. In this, today's religious right greatly resembles the cold, sterile, and doctrinaire religious leaders of Jesus' day whose rigidity and lack of understanding of the human condition Jesus preached against and separated himself from. For the substance of his message was a radical identification with the poor and downtrodden, the triumph of love over legalism, the hope of redemption from sin, the inclusion of all within that hope of redemption, and the promise of human and divine forgiveness.

Quite a number of prophets and religious leaders throughout the ages have demanded fundamentalist obedience of their followers. And if they did not, then their earliest disciples did. There is something inherent in discipleship that seems to demand strict adherence to the truths contained in their recollections of the teachings of that religion's founder. Interestingly enough, individuals as different as Thomas Jefferson and Leo Tolstoy believed it important to separate the teachings of Jesus from the interpretations placed on them by his disciples and later apostles, and each created his own version of the New Testament limited to the quotations from Jesus alone. The teachings of Jesus do not follow the pattern of most other prophets, teachers, and rabbis. They resist being reduced to rigid formulas and doctrinaire sets of rules.

Jesus sought to change the human heart. Though he urged his followers to obey ancient Hebraic law, he did not teach that obedient behavior guaranteed redemption or salvation. He taught that behavior resulted from redemption. "Where your treasure is, there will your heart be also." That which you value, that which you treasure, that is what determines who you really are. If you treasure wealth, your heart will be set on wealth. If you treasure power, your heart will be set on power. But, "blessed are they who hunger and thirst after righteousness, for they shall see God." Jesus did not see wealth and power as the means toward righteousness, he saw them as barriers to righteousness. You cannot hunger and thirst after wealth and power and achieve righteousness, for your heart will be absorbed with wealth and power.

Had Jesus been a fundamentalist, he would have preached only the Hebraic law as the path to salvation. But like all the great rabbis, he knew that obedience to the law without a loving heart is only the outward form of righteousness. And thus to the rich young man who told Jesus that he obeyed all the religious laws strictly, Jesus said, "Go and sell that thou hast and give to the poor, and you will have treasure in heaven." Adherence to the laws, strictness of behavior, did not guarantee the warmth of this man's heart.

Politically Jesus was a radical figure. Except to drive the money changers from the temple, he did not challenge established Jewish or Roman authority. He was critical of the sect of Pharisees for their hypocrisy, but he did not seek to destroy the temple or topple the government. "Render unto Caesar the things that are Caesar's," he replied to a critic who sought to catch him bringing religion into politics. "Render unto God the things that are God's." He was radical in the strict sense of the word; he got to the root of things. He was an itinerant Jewish peasant preacher at home more with ordinary people than the power structures of the day. But because he created a distinct, even unique set of values around the notion of the purity of one's heart, he forced people to question traditional values, to put their daily lives against the perspective of eternity, and to count what was truly important in life.

It is a great struggle to try to convert Jesus into a figure comfortable in today's conservative politics. He was not especially harsh with rich people, he simply pointed out the barrier their wealth represented to eternal life. He did not chastise the warrior, but he did bless the peacemaker. He did not curse the hypocrites, those who claimed religious superiority and acted otherwise, but he seemed to prefer the company of simpler and humbler folk. He did not condemn the winners in life's lottery, but he did single out for blessing the meek and the poor in spirit.

To make these observations is not to engage in partisanship. Both political parties have many rich people. Both political parties seek to demonstrate their commitment to national security through military strength. Both political parties have candidates who say one thing and do another. Both parties seek political power. It is in their very nature. And it must be said: both political parties have their share of sinners. But, as Franklin Roosevelt once said, "Divine justice weighs the sins of the cold-blooded and the sins of the warm-hearted on different scales."

And that is the point. It is not about who has the most wealth and who has the most power, at least where true faith is concerned. It is about the warmth of your heart, the generosity of your spirit, and the compassion of your soul. "What does it profit a man if he gain the whole world and lose his own soul?" If faith and values are to be imposed on politics, then whose faith and whose values? If it is the faith and values of Jesus, then American politics will have to change a great deal from what it is today. If the radical values preached by Jesus truly became the standard for twenty-first-century American politics, it would cause a social and political explosion of revolutionary proportions.

Is America really prepared to exhaust peaceful solutions before using military force to solve the world's problems? Are American politicians really prepared to raise taxes on wealth and create shelters for the homeless, provide decent health care for children and the elderly, and care for those without hope? Are we really prepared to force polluters to clean up their industrial waste to save God's green Earth? Are our sheltered politicians prepared to forego their trips to luxury golf courses in order to spend nights in the homes of the working poor? Will any political leader have the courage to say that executions are contrary to civilized society, the culture of life, and the teachings of Jesus? Is the president or even one member of Congress who advocated war in Iraq for faulty reasons prepared to fly to Baghdad to accompany the next planeload of coffins back to the their graves in the United States?

Those advocating more religious values in politics should proceed with utmost caution. If by faith they mean the Christian faith, and if by the Christian faith they mean the teachings of Jesus, *then they are advocating a wholesale revolution in political values in this country.* And not a revolution of the kind they have in mind, but a revolution of the human heart, a revolution that is directly contrary to the judgmentalism, absolutism, and elitism that characterize their actions. It would be a revolution more radical than they can possibly seem to imagine.

For the political-religious revival in America today is a revolution based on law. Its sense of justice is concerned with protection of wealth and property, not social justice for those left out. Its values are those of established power structures, not the values of the common good and the commonwealth. Its economics are those of greed and acquisition, not those of sharing or caring. Private charity, whether in the form of "faith-based initiatives" or "a thousand points of light," is blatantly insufficient to meet the needs of many millions of those left

> Fundamentalism is exclusionary, divisive, and destructive. Fundamentalism is ultimately incompatible with democratic principles of equality, justice, and fairness.

behind by our society and nothing but a convenient cover for absolving our society, through its government, of responsibility for seeking social justice. Its use of power is to go abroad seeking demons to destroy, not to make any serious effort to use American leadership to create new and better international structures to help solve global human needs.

Fundamentalism is a retreat from action and responsibility. It is a means of avoiding accountability. It says that all must adhere to our laws, our rules, our codes of conduct. It says that government must adopt our standards and measures and that we who guard the fundamentals will decide who is worthy to govern and who is not. Fundamentalism is exclusionary, divisive, and destructive. Fundamentalism is ultimately incompatible with democratic principles of equality, justice, and fairness. Religious fundamentalism, to paraphrase Emerson, writes no poetry, dreams no dreams, envisions no vision, lifts up no downtrodden.

Religious fundamentalism warms no heart.

Fundamentalism's rigidity can be traced to its dependence on law, orthodoxy, and conformity. Certainly organizations, including religious ones, must have structures and rules, if nothing else, to set out their distinctive features and to distinguish member believers from nonmember nonbelievers. By setting his teachings within the framework of the laws of Moses, Jesus acknowledged this fact and accepted the mainstream orthodoxy of his day. But, having accepted it, he then went well beyond it: "Think not that I am come to destroy the law or the prophets; I am come not to destroy, but to fulfil." He did not challenge the faith of Abraham; he expanded upon it in ways that are crucial to the issue of faith and politics in twenty-first-century America.

Jesus' essential message is that you can obey all the laws, conform to all the rules, practice all the rituals, and still fall short of the glory of God if you do not also possess a deep, abiding love for God and your fellow human beings that expresses itself in charity, mercy, and humility in everyday life. Over and over again, especially in dealing with those who obeyed the religious laws and rules yet found something missing in their lives, he taught that salvation lay in a purity of heart that willed one thing: a relationship with God that resulted in a changed life in relation to one's fellow human beings. He taught that law-based religion alone not only left the human heart longing for more, it also produced rigid, sterile, cold souls.

Here lies the danger for present-day fundamentalist Protestants who seek to occupy political power in order to impose their beliefs on others. By focusing on the civil laws of the United States, whether regarding reproductive rights, public funds for private religious activities, stem-cell research, AIDS prevention, contraceptive information, teaching of evolution, or restrictions on broadcasting and entertainment, the religious right seeks to make itself into an instrument of the state or to make the state an instrument of its beliefs, and it misses the essential power of Jesus' message. If you want to change human behavior, change the human heart.

And changing the human heart is the job of religion not the job of politics.

Jesus did not set out to create a faith in competition with Judaism, though that is what eventuated. Jesus did not set out to overthrow the Roman Empire, though (despite Constantine's adoption of the Christian faith whether through conviction or calculation) the empire did collapse. It is difficult if not impossible to find in the teachings of Jesus a mandate to occupy political power, even for what those who seek to do so consider righteous ends. The political activism of the religious right becomes even more problematic when it permits itself to be aligned with gun advocates, the death penalty, bans on school textbooks, and other highly divisive secular causes that either have nothing to do with the gospel of Jesus or are directly contrary to it. This is the danger in politicizing the Christian faith: direct involvement in secular politics inevitably enmeshes the religious believer in matters about which the creator of their faith had nothing to do or which are directly contradictory to his teachings.

Does anyone seriously believe that Jesus would have permitted himself to be involved in the gun ownership issues of his day? Instead, he deftly turned aside an entrapping question about paying taxes to Caesar. Does anyone seriously believe that Jesus would have actively supported the death penalty, particularly since it undercuts all he stood for? It is quite conceivable he would have taken a deeply spiritual stance on abortion, but, in keeping with similar issues of his day, he would have counseled any woman affected by the question to consult her spirit, her soul, and her heart, not her lawyer or political representative, before making that decision. There is no evidence he advocated enactment of a Roman law or even a Judaic law against taking such an action.

Beyond promoting obedience to the laws of men and questioning the limits of legislating moral behavior by Judaism, all Jesus' teachings trace to transformation of the human heart. There are certain things a loving heart will not and cannot do. It not only cannot kill, it cannot hate. It not only cannot steal, it cannot covet. It not only cannot coerce, it cannot wish to. This is the essential difference between faith and politics and the core reason why one should not be imposed on the other. Politics is a system for legislating human behavior. Faith is the process of changing the human heart. The human heart cannot be changed by legislation or coercion. This is the central reason why the efforts of the religious right to obtain its objectives through political means must fail. Either it must make its objectives political, which it has done, in which case it is no longer the activity of faith, or it must seek to change the human heart, which cannot be done by political means. One is an act of law. The other is an act of love.

This is also the basis for the fundamentally wise political act of separating the church from the state. Following Jesus, America's founders understood the difference between what was Caesar's and what was God's.

If the religious right is genuinely serious about changing the laws of the United States, it should have sufficient confidence in the righteousness of its beliefs and the causes that it will seek to change human hearts in the belief that those changed human hearts will agree with its doctrines, become active politically, and come to represent a political majority. There is in fact a moral majority in America—the vast majority of Americans are moral—but that majority has not automatically accepted the political positions of those who claim to represent it. That has been the frustration of the religious right. It assumed that the majority of Americans were moral, a correct assumption, but then mistakenly concluded that to be moral meant natural acceptance of *its* definitions of what constituted morality. In this it has been mistaken.

Faced with this reality, elements of the religious right then organized to occupy a position of power within one political party, fundamentally changing, over the course of a decade, what had been a libertarian, tolerant, and moderate party into one primarily concerned with imposing upon the nation conservative religious principles, limiting reproductive rights, perpetuating the death penalty, publicly supporting private religious activities, and instigating a preemptive, crusader foreign policy designed to remake the world in America's image. It is impossible to find justification for any of these political positions in the teachings of Jesus or even, for that matter, in traditional American conservatism.

Virtually all Christians, whether politically conservative or otherwise, agree on an inherent tendency toward sinfulness in human nature. Two millennia have been devoted to defining what is and what is not sinful. The church in which I was brought up, as I have mentioned, believed dancing to be sinful and, as I have also mentioned, Catholics of that relatively recent era believed eating meat on Friday was sinful. Great Christian schisms have been caused by differences over what were and were not sins on the margins of the core Judeo-Christian ethic. Times change. And those differences will continue so long as times change. That does not mean that basic morality changes. Killing is a sin. Stealing is a sin. Adultery is a sin. The difficulty always has been and always will be in defining sinfulness beyond the traditional boundaries of a religious consensus on sinful behavior.

Defining illegality is the undertaking of politics because it involves human conduct. Defining sinfulness is the undertaking of religion because it involves the human heart.

And that fact as much as anything else warrants appreciation for Jesus' counsel that we not judge others. This admonition, occurring on several occasions in his teachings, leads us to understand the importance that he attached to reticence in judgment. Jesus was not preaching relativism. He was preaching the fallibility of even the most righteous believer in understanding the circumstances of another human's condition and behavior. He preached a fundamental truth: each of us is a sinner, none of us is sufficiently perfect to have the moral authority to judge another, and none of us can know the interior of another human's heart. He is not against judgment. He is against judgment based on imperfect knowledge. Therefore, God alone can be the judge of the human soul.

Even more important, at the core of the Christian faith is not judgment but forgiveness. Jesus taught that as God can forgive sin, humans can forgive one another. It is the fundamental doctrine of redemption. The sinner can be redeemed. Once a sinner does not mean always a sinner. People must forgive one another because all are imperfect. But people cannot redeem the souls of other men. Only God can do that. Today the religious right is advocating judgment and not forgiveness and is therefore setting itself up as the arbiter of human conduct beyond the scope of the core Judeo-Christian beliefs. By failing to adhere to Jesus' teaching that we judge not, the political-religious right assumes the role of the Old Testament judges, umpires of the rules of conduct, and therefore morally superior to those they judge.

As I might respect individual religious figures much more conservative than I, and even possibly more free of sin, I know of none of them qualified to act as moral judge over me or anyone else. "Judge not that ye be not judged." Jesus' insight is a penetrating one. Anyone assuming to judge the interior morality of others opens himself or herself to examination, and to pass muster he or she must be without flaw. Do not try to remove the mote from your brother's eye when you have a beam in your own. ("How wilt thou say to thy brother, Let me pull out the mote out of thine eye; and, behold, a beam is in thine own eye?") It is simply impossible to find authority in the Scriptures for the use of the political process to impose by law one's particular view of contested moral and social issues on all others. A church or religious organization may certainly press its scriptural interpretations, points of view, and doctrines on its members and applicants for membership. That is vastly different from entering the political arena, by capturing a political party, as a means of imposing those interpretations, views, and doctrines on an entire nation.

For to do so is to invite commission of other sins against which Jesus warned: the sins of arrogance, self-righteousness, and hypocrisy. Being judgmental, the political-religious right sets itself up as exclusionary. Sinners need not apply. To believe oneself to be of the elect is to possess a Calvinistic certainty that produces absolutism. Those absolutely convinced of their own righteousness, especially those with a predestinarian belief in the "elect" and the deterministic separation of the saved from the damned, find very little common cause with those who do not share the clarity of their convictions. Once again, however, exclusivity runs counter to the inclusiveness of the Christian gospel and to Jesus' own practices. Jesus repeatedly sought out the common people and invited association with those considered impure—including lepers, adulterers, and the demon-possessed—by the religious institutions of the day. Those whom Jesus warned about hurdles barring entry to the kingdom of heaven were those with wealth and particularly those whose material wealth represented their principle preoccupation. Hypocrites, those professing belief but without genuine compassion, came in for his scorn. And he taught that rigid adherence to religious law without a warm heart was form without substance. Jesus blessed the meek, the peacemakers, the poor in spirit, those who mourn, and the needy, not categories one thinks of in describing the early twenty-first-century religious right in America.

There is, of course, nothing that should prevent members of the religious right from participating in American politics in any way they see fit, including occupation of dominant positions in one political party, and this essay is not an argument against that participation. They may, if they achieve sufficient power, nominate candidates who pass muster with them, including candidates for president; dictate the terms and substance of the party's platforms; preach, if they so choose, against candidates from any other party; lobby for legislation at the local, state, and federal level; and take any other positions of political power they wish to take—so long as they are open and honest (as some have not been) about who they are and what their agendas are.

What the fundamentalist Protestant conservative wing of the broader Christian faith must not do in pursuing its political agenda, however, is to claim exclusive representation of the teachings of Jesus, the historic traditions of the Christian church, or the definitive standards to qualify for Christian forgiveness. The political agenda of the religious right must not be confused with what should be its primary obligation: to preach the central truths of the Christian faith. One does not preclude the other, but the latter must not be imposed on the former.

The cross of Jesus is not a piece of jewelry to be worn around the neck. It is an awful burden borne on one's soul. It requires the bearer not only to obey ancient religious laws but, even more importantly, to carry out Jesus' teachings. It symbolizes not pride and arrogance but humility and service.

The poet John Keats wrote that he had "an awful warmth about my heart, like a load of immortality." Not only does this describe Jesus, but it also should describe all those who seek to follow him. Very little of this awful warmth is exhibited by figures of the religious right who seek political power or by the rigid politicians who, cynically or not, seek to use religion to promote their own careers.

When their hearts experience this awful warmth, perhaps then they will be qualified to preach to us. But perhaps then, simple humility will prevent them from seeking to do so.

Retreat from Enlightenment

The quarrel of the early twenty-first-century American religious-political right is not, as it argues, with liberalism; its quarrel is with the Enlightenment. For it was the English and Scottish Enlightenment that liberated America's founders to hold to traditional, though largely Protestant, Christianity and, at the same time, pursue the ideal of knowledge, critical learning, the analytical method, science and scientific investigation, and, in Jefferson's phrase, "the progress of the human mind." The Enlightenment above all else liberated human learning, and, with the Reformation that preceded it, liberated politics and political systems from the confines of the medieval church, priestly control of knowledge, mythology and mystery, and religious cultism. The key to the survival of democracy for Jefferson was not the influence of the church but the liberation of the human mind by broad-based *public*—not parochial—education.

The founders of the nation and most of its subsequent leaders have seen no conflict between reason and faith, between belief in a Supreme Creator and the requirement for critical and analytical thought in democratic governance. No founder who comes to mind, including those most adamant in their faith, claimed to be so directly attuned to divine wisdom that he found curiosity, learning, debate, and rationality to be unnecessary. Faith in God does not guarantee special insights on governance in the secular world, especially when those claiming the faith act contrary to history and experience.

A prophet of the Renaissance, Niccolò Machiavelli, knew what he was doing when he counseled the Prince to take the place of the Priest, to condition his followers by creating awe and wonder. As much as perhaps anyone else, Machiavelli secularized politics by having the state, in the form of the Prince, replace the church, in the form of the Priest, and thereby began to legitimize secular governance.

Today's religious right has in mind to return America to the pre-Enlightenment age, an age in which the church, in this case in the form of one wing of evangelical Protestantism, dictates terms to the political process and sets the boundaries of what can and cannot be legislated and regulated by the state.

A spectacular undertaking of this sort requires a breathtaking certainty acquired only through divine guidance. If, as President Bush has suggested on more than one occasion, his policies are acquired directly from God, this helps explain the absence of curiosity, the resistance to debate, the lack of interest in new facts and information, the disinterest in compromise or the need for consensus, and disdain for what is called "the reality-based community." To possess absolute certainty is to obtain

> **Faith in God does not guarantee special insights on governance in the secular world, especially when those claiming the faith act contrary to history and experience.**

release from the democratic process itself. It has been some time, certainly quite a number of centuries, since the world witnessed a self-proclaimed empire of the righteous whose policies are made in heaven and carried out by the servants of the Lord, servants who happen, in this case, to possess the mightiest military power in human history.

This prospect might or might not hold concern for nations of other faiths or secular states not claiming divine direction. But it certainly holds little attraction for those of us steeped in the democratic republican traditions restored by the Enlightenment.

If the American people come to believe that this, or any, president is immediately directed by God in the performance of his duties, then our good fortune would be sufficiently spectacular to insist that the United States Constitution be amended to permit unlimited terms in office. I, for one, however, would feel more comfortable, even with a president possessing a hotline to heaven, if that individual read a little more history, asked more questions, sought advice from a few more people who see things differently, or spent some time in a few more foreign cultures.

Reason is not the enemy of religion, unless that religion insists on national policies contrary to reason. Aren't we all deeply affected by our deeply held beliefs, one might ask, and don't those beliefs influence all else we do in life? Are not the political activists of the religious right merely performing their duties as citizens to participate in the nation's public life? And if they participate in public life, will they not necessarily promote their deeply held beliefs? Of course, is the answer to all such questions. But all this is a far cry from churches, religious organizations, and wealthy contributors forming networks of lobbying organizations, systematically occupying positions of power in a national political party, demanding inclusion of its agenda in that party's platform, vetoing candidates for elective office at all levels who do not

> **Reason is not the enemy of religion, unless that religion insists on national policies contrary to reason.**

subscribe to that agenda, insisting on approval of federal judicial appointments, formulating that party's electoral strategy, cynically promoting divisive social referenda (such as anti–gay marriage initiatives) as a means of motivating its members to vote, all for the purpose of imposing its religious agenda on the body politic. But, you say, isn't this simply clever politics? Indeed it is. It is not, however, what Jesus taught.

As a candidate for national office at a time when the religious right was beginning to organize its influence on the political process, I was occasionally asked, though not to any extent that politicians are asked today, how my religious beliefs influenced my political beliefs, and I was occasionally urged by political advisors to refer more often to my religious family, college, divinity school education, and personal beliefs. Although I did so when it seemed appropriate to explain why I felt deeply about a particular issue or when asked directly about my background and fundamental beliefs, I chose not to use any of this background as a means of seeking votes or support, even when it might have been advantageous to do so. This was not because I found it embarrassing in any way whatsoever, because I felt it might seem quaint, or because I was concerned about alienating voters of other faiths. It was simply because my faith was *my* faith, a personal matter, and, though it did heavily condition my political beliefs in ways explained in this essay, I wanted people to support or not support me because of those political beliefs and not because of my faith. Nor did I feel that I was on a mission to impose my religious beliefs on a multicultural, religiously pluralistic nation. When it was an issue in his presidential campaign, John Kennedy took exactly the same position, neither seeking to hide his Catholicism nor to use it to seek Catholic votes. This was a position the founders of our nation would have understood.

That fact does not suggest that America's founders were not themselves deeply and profoundly influenced by their Judeo-Christian heritage and the Western Christian traditions. They did, officially and unofficially, acknowledge their dependence on their Creator, Divine Providence, and a Supreme Being. But they also repeatedly resisted any temptation to insert Christian doctrines into the new constitutional democracy, once again proving that it is possible to be a believing politician without also becoming a political evangelist.

Those who claim the right to power through divine guidance today, however, can never be satisfied with partial success. Having achieved electoral victories in the White House and Congress, it is no accident that the religious right now turns its attention to the remaining branch of government, the judicial system. If federal courts interpret the Constitution and laws of the United States in ways that frustrate the political and social agenda of the religious right, then its solution is to remake the courts by limiting qualification for the judiciary to those who accept its agenda. The whole process, whether regarding the presidency, Congress, or the judiciary, is to limit what the national government can do and to dictate what it *must* do socially according to the restrictive beliefs of the religious minority. However else this counterrevolution is described, it is most certainly one that rejects moderate consensus and secular governance in favor of a narrowly religious interpretation of reality and the proper functions of the state. In the simplest terms, this is an attempt to make the state subservient to religion, in this case not even state religion but a narrow sectarian religion out to restore to itself the power and influence of the medieval church.

Nor is the power it seeks restricted to the cultural realm. In the process of replacing democratic debate with sectarian certainty, the religious right has made common

cause with those who have their own separate, mostly economic, quarrels with government. Since the age of the New
Deal these quarrels have included opposition to social programs involving income redistribution, regulation of environmental pollution, protection of workers' rights and
workplace safety, and a wide range of efforts to achieve
social progress. On the other hand, by urging greater state
dictation of social mores as defined by fundamentalist religion, the religious right has alienated, and rightly so, the libertarian wing of American conservatism.

The net result of the marriage of the revivalist right
with neo-conservatism is to produce a polity based on pre-
Enlightenment divine right, a pre–New Deal, laissez-faire
economy, and a role for America in the world more remi-
niscent of the twelfth-century Crusades than twentieth-
century democratic alliances. In an age of great uncertainty
produced by national boundaries eroded by global trade and
tidal waves of information, by failed states and proliferation
of weapons of mass destruction, by terrorism carried out by
stateless nations, and by the collapse of old certainties, there
is every cause for seeking spiritual guidance and transcen-
dent truths. They will offer little hope or security, however,
if they require us to abandon thought, reason, the lessons of
history, and the accumulated wisdom of centuries.

In the revolutionary era of the early twenty-first century,
we do not require less enlightenment. We require more.

Beliefs, Values, and Social Justice

The debate, if one wishes to call it that, in recent national elections over faith and values rarely if ever specified faith in what or whose values, leaving space for everyone to fill in their own meanings, beliefs, creeds, and prejudices. Trained in the evangelical Christian tradition, my *faith* came to be centered on the teachings of Jesus. I *value* courage, justice, honor, integrity, and duty. These values were shaped by my religious tradition, the ethics learned from a rooted if very modest family, the lessons in history and civics from the public schools in Ottawa, Kansas, and wise teachers such as Professor Prescott Johnson. In all this I am little different from the vast majority of ethically sound, morally decent Americans who have solid values, most of whom possess a religious faith of some kind, and more than a few of whom are tempted to sin.

I find the core of Jesus' teachings in the Sermon on the Mount in the fifth chapter of Saint Matthew's gospel. In this sermon, Jesus sets out his own values for his disciples and the attending multitudes by describing what qualities and actions deserve to be blessed and, by implication, what qualities do not. He starts with the poor in spirit, "for theirs," he says, "is the kingdom of heaven." Who exactly the poor in spirit are is not set forth. We can imagine it includes, at least, all those genuinely saddened by misfortune, or those who are lonely or abandoned, or those with little hope, or those who simply cannot cope with human cruelty. He then blesses those who mourn, "for they shall be comforted." He promises divine comfort for those experiencing the loss of a family member or friend or perhaps for those who mourn for other reasons, possibly for the injustices of their age. He says that the meek are blessed, "for they shall inherit the earth." This blessing has always seemed strange to me in that Jesus minimized earthly rewards and, as in this sermon, encouraged attention to heavenly rewards. Perhaps he means inheritance of the good things of the Earth: love and friendships, compassion and human warmth, the beauties of nature, the inspiration of a courageous deed. "Those who hunger and thirst after righteousness" are blessed, for, he promises, they will be filled with the righteousness they long for. Though Jesus does not say when, I like to believe he left open the possibility of their longings being met here on Earth. Perhaps the righteousness he promises will produce a just society and a righteous nation. Let us hope. And those who show mercy are blessed because they will receive mercy. Perhaps the clearest of the beatitudes promises mercy to the merciful. By implication it suggests that those who place legal justice over mercy may receive little mercy when their time of judgment comes and they find themselves in need of mercy. Jesus' time, much like our own, was not wanting in strict legal justice with its punishments and penalties. But also like our own, it was noticeably short of mercy.

There is a special blessing for peacemakers, "for they shall be called the children of God." One cannot help but think of someone like General Roméo Dallaire, a hero who struggled without success to save hundreds of thousands of Rwandan Tutsis from slaughter. He now lives with this burden, but perhaps he, and too few like him, truly are children of God. What a profound blessing. And perhaps it is profound because it is so rare. Equally special is the blessing for the pure in heart, "for they shall see God." Without being overly judgmental, the rarity of the pure heart suggests that the audience with God will be small. I have known a very few people whose hearts I thought to be pure. But only God can judge.

Jesus' final blessing is reserved for those who are persecuted for the sake of righteousness. Here he seems to prefigure the fate of the early apostles, some of whom, like him, would be crucified for preaching their gospel. Some New Testament scholars have suggested that Matthew may have been tempted to add this blessing later to encourage the disciples and apostles, for he has Jesus expand on the prospects of those persecuted for righteousness sake, saying that they are to be particularly blessed when they are reviled and evilly accused for his sake. He concludes by telling them to rejoice and be glad, for they will receive great rewards in heaven as did the prophets who suffered similar persecutions before them. Following these beatitudes Jesus addresses either all those included in those blessings, or the disciples, or the multitude. In some ways it seems as if it must be the first. For he calls them the salt of the earth and the light of the world and urges them to show their light "like a city set upon a hill." Jesus then proceeds to say that he has not come to destroy the law, the ancient commandments, but to fulfill them, and he preaches at some length as to how his followers are to go beyond the strict limits and narrow, legalistic interpretations of the laws to "turn the other cheek."

It is not the purpose of this essay to provide one person's biblical interpretations but merely to give some specificity to undefined terms such as "faith" and "values" where I, as one individual, am concerned. It is to be hoped that present-day political figures who use these undefined terms might seek to do likewise, that is to tell us what exactly they have faith in and what their values are. In my own case, my values are not limited to the Sermon on the Mount. I believe that God created the Earth and all that is in it. I believe we are encouraged to develop the Earth's resources to the degree that those resources are not exhausted and thus denied future generations, to the degree that their development does not irrevocably contaminate God's earth, air, and water, and to the degree that our use of the Earth's resources represents wise stewardship.

Otherwise, I believe that plundering the Earth's resources for greedy purposes and personal wealth is immoral. It may also be sinful, but that is for God to decide. It certainly should also be illegal, but today it too often is not. The religious right, at least until recently, has not been heard to speak out against this immorality. In fact, what comments have been heard from the religious right on the resources of nature have almost all been in favor of immediate development of those resources by this generation for its own use, enjoyment, and, especially, profit. Their values apparently do not include stewardship, generational accountability, or respect for God's creation.

Despite efforts to minimize, marginalize, or discredit the problems of climate change and global warming, at the very least our reckless consumption raises serious questions about the relationship of human beings to the natural

world. Here people of faith should make a contribution to a
serious public discussion. That contribution should be to
state what our various religious heritages teach us about
how we are to manage our natural resources, including most
of all our earth, air, and water, in the most ethical and moral
way. I am heavily influenced by the ideal of stewardship, that
we are caretakers of our natural environment and must
manage it in ways that do least harm to other human beings
and to the exquisitely intricate natural environment itself.
Others may place immediate profit on a higher scale. I
believe in intergenerational accountability, that we have ethical and moral obligations to future generations to pass on a
world in better condition than we found it and to preserve
our natural heritage. Others may believe the end is near and
the future therefore matters for little. I believe the Earth
belongs to God and not to humankind and that our duty is
to care for what God has given us. Others may believe that
the Earth is simply a collection of products to be consumed,
some sort of gigantic Wal-Mart.

Except for apocalyptic Christianity, which believes
there may be no tomorrow, virtually every religion in the
world places importance on protec-
tion of nature and on family and
societal obligation to the previous
and to the next generations. Some
religions, including the religions of
Native Americans, go so far as to
believe that nature cannot be separate from God, that God is in nature.
Of course we sophisticated modernists know better.
Otherwise, to abuse nature would be to abuse God.

> How can one claim to
> believe in God's cre-
> ation and still place
> profit over protection
> and preservation?

Issues such as protection of nature and care for the
poor illustrate the complexity and occasional hypocrisy of

"faith-based" politics, campaigns based on "values," and efforts to import religious doctrines into the art of politics. How can one claim to believe in God's creation and still place profit over protection and preservation? How can one claim faith and values and show so little concern for our legacy to our children and grandchildren? How can one claim to be a follower of Jesus and not act on his many admonitions in society's arena? How can one condemn the sins committed by members of the disfavored political party but be silent when the same sins are committed by members of the favored party? Indeed, how can religious judgment all seem to be rendered against one political party? The "values" employed are very partisan values. All this religious partisanship is a very short step away from preaching that Jesus was a member of one political party.

This kind of political activity may encourage one party and its candidates, but it certainly does nothing to further the gospel of Jesus.

Thomas Paine put it a different way: "Any system of religion that has anything in it that shocks the mind of a child," he wrote, "cannot be a true system."

Jesus taught in parables, and the one of greatest influence on my life is the parable of the landowner and his three stewards found in the gospel of Matthew. Before going on a trip, the master gives each of them some talents: to one of them five talents, to another two, and to the third steward one talent. He then instructs them to administer their talents wisely. After a time, he returns and asks each of the stewards for an accounting. The stewards with five and two talents have invested them wisely and doubled their value, and the landowner says, "Well done, good and faithful servants." The third servant, the steward with one talent, reports that he buried it in order to protect it. To him the employer is angry. He has not done his best. He has not tried. He has not used his talent to the best of his ability.

Several things, I gather, are to be taken from this lesson. We are not all given the same talents, but that is not what is important to God. What is important is what we do with what we are given, for we are meant to do the best we can with whatever talents we are given. I can think of nothing greater than to make beautiful music or to conduct an orchestra that makes beautiful music. But, alas, I was not given that talent. There are many other things, in athletics, in oratory, in scholarship, I would like to have accomplished, but I was not given those talents. Much to my surprise, and with no natural advantage or family heritage, I found a small talent in the political arena. I sought to use it as well and as wisely, to the limits of that talent, as I could. Though I never felt a destiny to be president, I endeavored to achieve that goal for the purpose of bringing the Cold War to an end, revitalizing and expanding education in America, and creating a new environmental ethic, among many other things, but that was not meant to be. (For my own failings in this regard, I would simply ask the same forgiveness from those who might question my legitimacy to write this essay that they have granted our current president for his previous transgressions.)

The parable of the talents suggests to me a standard for America in the twenty-first century. What if we had a national goal to enable and empower every American to use his or her talents to the fullest? You may say that this goal is already the genius of America, that this country automatically and naturally provides that empowerment in its economic and political systems, that many individual examples exist of the triumph of this goal. And the citation of those examples, of the Abraham Lincolns, the Isaac Sterns, the Jonas Salks, all do support the genius of America. But surely there are many others, hundreds of thousands if not millions of others, children in ghettos, young people forced by lack of support to drop out of school, ambitious students without the means to obtain higher education, adults trapped in unproductive jobs, all of whom possess a talent, or five. In a capitalist system, we are all on our own, with the possible support of private charity in a "faith-based" society, and many with talent do succeed. But I have an idea that there are many others who are denied by bitter, insurmountable circumstance the chance to put their talents to use.

I wish our values included making sure that everyone in our country had a chance to use their talents to the fullest. It is certainly within our capacity to do so. For those with natural opportunity, especially those with inherited wealth, to pretend that everyone has an equal chance is to cling to an illusion. A wise and beneficent government would knock down barriers and expand preparation, particularly for the young, to take advantage of what this great nation has to offer. Such a national effort would truly be values based.

My values include a caring society that seeks to use the instruments of government to help children in poverty, the elderly in need, the homeless, and the jobless. Those values are directly and immediately shaped by my family and church, by my reading of the Bible, and by my total heritage. They are largely the reason I became active in public life. These are social goals shaped by religious values. I am as compelled by my religious beliefs toward my liberal political values as members of the religious right are compelled to their conservative values. We all might profitably ponder why the same God would plant such equally strong yet contrary beliefs in different people claiming the same faith. The religious right does not agree with my social and political values, though I have yet to hear members of the religious right reconcile their opposition to social justice with the gospel of Jesus. In espousing my social values, however, I rarely invoke my religious beliefs to justify those values. To me they were and are what a decent and just society should do for its members in need.

My social values are shaped by my religious beliefs, but I do not need to impose my religious beliefs on others to promote my social values.

Micah 6:8

"What does the Lord require of thee, but to do justly, and to love mercy, and to walk humbly with thy God." Justice, mercy, and humility. These are indeed values by which to live. They are even better values by which to govern. But each is in short supply these days. Somehow we can assume that the prophet Micah did not have in mind legal justice. To "do justly" seems to suggest living fairly and decently and treating all with respect. To "love mercy" prefigures Jesus' blessing on the merciful who themselves will receive mercy. One of our values should be to create a merciful society. Then we could live in the hope of receiving mercy ourselves. And to walk humbly with God means not only to be humble before God but also to exhibit humility toward others, as a person walking with God would do. There is little to suggest in our political, commercial, or cultural worlds that we live in an age that values humility.

A just, merciful, and humble person is not a judgmental person or a person who seeks to impose his or her values on others, especially through the use of political power and influence. Yet that is what the religious right, the merger of fundamentalist religion and rightist ideology, seeks to do. This new political and religious orthodoxy seems less interested in doing justly and more interested in forcing others to accept its doctrinaire system of legal justice. It exhibits little interest in mercy but rather is merciless to those with whom it disagrees. And as for humility, there is but little. If one single thing characterizes the religious and political figures of the right, it is the absence of any sense of humility.

If nothing else, however, the merger of fundamentalist Protestantism and neo-conservatism and the occupation by both of one political party has brought to the surface yet again the abiding and real question of the relationship of religion, or, as it is now called, "faith," to democratic politics in America. It is an interesting and an important question. There is nothing to fear in raising this question, particularly if it is done so in a thoughtful and civilized manner. In the meantime, and while that debate goes on, Micah has offered some simple guiding principles for us. America, and individual Americans if they so choose, should do justly, should love mercy, and should walk humbly with God, in whatever form they see God.

We should not fear a nation that follows these principles. We should seek it. Nations can seek to be righteous, in the deepest meaning of that term, without becoming self-righteous. For only God judges who is and who is not righteous, and we should conduct ourselves in such ways that we may earn a favorable judgment. Nations can exhibit mercy and ours should seek to do so. America was not created to be the world's avenging angel, and it is for God alone to "trample out the vineyards where the grapes of wrath are stored." We should not mistake our human swords for "His terrible swift sword." And we should walk humbly. Much more than for all our material wealth and our lifestyles, the peoples of the world respect and envy our principles, including our constitutional freedoms, the rule of law, the balance of governmental powers, the freedom of speech and worship, and the rest of our Bill of Rights. We should observe our own principles and seek, with humility, to live up to them and to have the courage, integrity, and greatness to admit when we have failed to do so.

Were we to choose to do justly, to love mercy, and to walk humbly with God, we would be well on our way toward becoming the kind of righteous nation the religious right claims to desire. We would not need for those in that group to assume superior political authority and dictate terms to all the rest of us. A first step in this direction might be for members of the religious right to confess that demonization of American liberalism is an unjust and unfair political tactic, unworthy of those who claim to be followers of Jesus. Some of Jesus' teachings were conservative in many ways, but quite a number of them, by current standards, would also have to be judged quite liberal. In any case, I seriously doubt that Jesus contemplated whether he was a conservative or a liberal, categories much misused by political pundits and practitioners.

Nothing short of a cataclysm of gigantic proportions would truly cause the great United States of America to become the theocracy the religious right seems to have in mind. It would require a wave of significant terrorist attacks for Americans to trade their freedoms to authoritarian security agencies for state protection and security. It would require the collapse of a debt- and deficit-ridden economy for Americans to succumb to a judicial system presided over by rigid ideologues. It would require a reign of the kind of fear Franklin Roosevelt warned us against to surrender the instruments of democratic government to the ministers and religious lobbying groups of one wing of one element of one religion.

Though some already fear such a thing, the vast majority of Americans will not let this happen. Deep within our
souls is an understanding of the reasons our founders
wanted us to be free to worship, or not worship, as we
choose, free of government influence, and wanted our government to be free of the political influence of any religion.
If either of these circumstances were to change, then
America would be a very different country from the one it
has been for almost 225 years.

Justice, mercy, and humility seem to also encompass
tolerance, understanding, patience, forbearance, and mag-
nanimity, qualities (perhaps values) one would not say particularly characterize our age. If we could get the "values"
politicians to be somewhat more specific, then we might
have a serious national debate about our values and how
they should impact our politics. I, for one, would welcome a
national consensus that caused our policies and political
decisions to be guided by tolerance, forbearance, and mag-
nanimity. But, once again, I somehow do not think those are
the values this code word implies.

Perhaps, after all, America's greatest need today is a visit
from the prophet Micah.

God and Caesar

Someday God, in His wisdom, may decide to govern a human nation. If so, He will decide which one and how it shall be governed. If He needs any help, He knows how to reach us.

My guess is, if He does require our help, it will not be in the form of the religious figures seeking political power in America today. If, however, I am wrong, and if He selects them to govern America, He will surely understand if a few of us go in search of a democracy in which to live.

Until then, we will have to struggle on, guided by our heterogeneous religious backgrounds, our consensus moral values, and the guidance we received more than two centuries ago from men and women steeped in the Enlightenment tradition, all of which pretty much agree that Caesar rules the secular realm and God the spiritual. If God decides to replace Caesar, He can do it without our help.

Caesar, of course, is but a figure of speech for all human governments. We in America believe, with considerable justification, that we have the most evolved form of government, though it was the inimitable Churchill himself (who seemed sometimes impishly tempted to act as if he were God) who decreed that democracy was the worst form of government, except for all the others.

The religious right in early twenty-first-century America barely conceivably could prevail, against all democratic odds, in imposing its will on our government and society. If so, we will no longer be the America of the past 225 years. We will be distinctly something else. It will be some modern form of pre-Enlightenment, medieval theocracy, and it will not be attractive to behold.

Senators will consult with designated clerics before voting or introducing legislation. Presidents will appoint only those judges approved by the same clerics. (Imagine that.) Cabinet officers will each have their own liaison officers to the established churches and religious lobbying organizations, presuming their political advisors do not already perform that function. Government regulations that have any social consequences will have to be preapproved by the official established church. Public broadcasting, and probably privately produced entertainment, will require approval of content that clerics might find offensive. The implications go on, and clearly they are profound. We are rapidly advancing, often covertly, toward all these things.

This is not a pretty picture because democratic politics, the realm of Caesar, involve compromise and consensus while religion, the realm of God, is premised upon absolutes, and divine ones at that. The only times in human history when the absolutes of organized religion have been imposed on governments and political structures, theocracy, government by the church, has resulted. Democratic politics requires the ability and the willingness to negotiate, to bargain, to persuade, and, yes, even to trade. Systems founded on absolutes do not permit this. Given their insistence on divine guidance, there is nothing to discuss, let alone compromise about. The very idea of compromise is anathema to those who believe they possess divine truth and direction.

And this fact, more than any other, accounts for the sclerosis afflicting American politics today—the unwillingness of those claiming access to divine truth to participate in the kind of constructive compromise that makes democratic politics possible at all.

It is one thing for a secular society and its government to invoke God's blessing on a political cause, particularly in wartime. It is quite another thing for a nation to go to war because, it argues, God commanded it. This is the crusader mentality. President George W. Bush briefly referred to the second war with Iraq as a "crusade" until he was told that, in the Arab Middle East, this was a notion with an unpleasant history attached. Democratic governments have no business invoking religious inspiration for foreign military adventures. We did not defeat Germany in World War II to make it a Christian nation. It already was (to a fault). Likewise, and even more so, democratic governments, including the government of the United States, have no business passing laws or pursuing policies determining what its citizens may or may not do because they are instructed to do so by one wing of a larger wing of one religion.

Democracy only works if it fosters compromise. This is particularly true in mass democracies of 300 million people from pluralistic faiths, a multitude of backgrounds, and of many nationalities. The range of ideologies in America is vast, but its politics polarize around liberal and conservative dispositions. From a number of years of experience in the Senate chamber, I know that our system only works when it encourages compromise between liberals and conservatives, and it works almost not at all when it does not. Recently it

Democracy only works if it fosters compromise. This is particularly true in mass democracies of 300 million people from pluralistic faiths, a multitude of backgrounds, and of many nationalities.

has not been working well, in part because the willingness to compromise is quickly disappearing. This circumstance has been created in no small measure by the introduction of absolutes, especially "faith-based" absolutes, into a political system where no single group gets everything that it demands and often does not even get one thing it wants unblemished by compromise.

The religious right simply cannot control the political process in America. That is my absolute.

Intimidation, huffing and puffing, demonization of liberals, foot stomping, ultimatums, tantrums, and thunderous denunciations do not ultimately work in a democracy, and they will not work much longer in the American democracy.

The time will come, and it will come sooner rather than later, when the ponderous pendulum of American public opinion begins its return to its inevitable moderate center. Politicians hiding behind the robes of ministers, policy makers courting a vociferous religious element, adventurers cloaking foreign military ventures in the crusader's rhetoric, political manipulators cynically using public fears to turn out voters all will be swept back into our nation's nooks and crannies from whence they emerged. This *must* happen, because America cannot be governed otherwise.

Benjamin Disraeli, who knew a thing or two about religion and politics, summarized his views in a fictional dialogue:

"Sensible men are all of the same religion."

"And pray, what is that?"

"Sensible men never tell."

"Render unto Caesar that which is Caesar's and render unto God that which is God's." With some notable exceptions, the United States is an upright nation, it is a moral nation, it is a decent, open, and fair nation. Most of all, and at our best, we are a principled nation. Though an occasional revival of religion certainly cannot hurt, we are not a particularly sinful nation, certainly not when displayed against the panoply of sinful nations.

We do best among ourselves and in our dealings with others when we live up to our principles. That is more difficult than it may seem, because our founders purposefully set our principles high. They intended the United States to be exceptional, and they hoped that Divine Providence intended us to be so. But they knew full well that we would have to struggle against the forces of greed, selfishness, corruption, and human folly to even hope to live up to the extraordinarily high standards of justice, equality, fairness, honor, and the common good that they established.

Our founders knew that we would be governed by fallible human beings because it was only fallible human beings from among whom we could select our leaders. They did not believe that human fallibility in the political sphere could be corrected by opening the corridors of power to ministers, priests, and rabbis. To the contrary, to turn over the reigns of government to religious leaders could lead to one of only two destructive consequences: we would become a theocratic principality familiar to old Europe or religion would be totally discredited and taken over by the state.

It is not blasphemy to thank God for their wisdom. That wisdom has saved us before and, if we let ourselves hear it, it will, I firmly believe, save us yet again.

I have been so greatly privileged that sometimes it almost makes me weep. My story is not all that much different from other Americans born into humble circumstances to upright parents and blessed by fortune. I have experienced economic depression and I have been blessed with a comfortable living. I have attended small-town public schools and I have graduated from great universities of the world. I started without political advantage and I have approached the gates of the American presidency. I have driven spikes into countless railroad ties and I have been the guest of kings.

To justify this extraordinary privilege and to be accountable to my Creator, I have tried to make the utmost use of what talent I was given.

My greatest privilege is that I am an American. That means that no man or woman can tell me what to believe. No minister, priest, or rabbi can dictate my political principles. No religious figure or organization can claim control of my government. No sect or church can replace the constitutional democracy that countless American patriots have given their lives to protect and preserve.

I believe that America still has a destiny. Whether that destiny is divinely dictated, neither I nor anyone else can ever say or ever know. I do believe that America's unrealized destiny has to do with achieving social justice in our own society, leading the world through a time of great revolution, setting higher standards for the protection of our Earth, raising the standard of human rights for all, and calling forth the better angels of our nature. God's work is never done and, as John Kennedy said, "here on Earth, God's work must truly be our own."

In the words of our Republic's greatest hymn, "Our God is marching on." And so is the United States of America.

— Gary Hart
Kittredge, Colorado